MsGeezerette's Journey Thru Baby Boomer Land at the Speed of Wrinkles

Michele Mikesic Bender

Copyright © 2019 Michele Mikesic Bender

All rights reserved.

ISBN: 1726037746
ISBN-13: 978-1726037747

DEDICATION

I dedicate this book to all the precious souls, living and departed, whose lives touched mine and who shared adventures and milestones in "Boomer-Land" with me.
Without them, my head would not be filled with these treasured memories..

CONTENTS

	Acknowledgments	i
	Forward	1
1	Kid Stuff	4
2	Adolescent Antics	14
3	Meet the Folks	27
4	Heaven Smiled	38
5	In Sickness and in Health	45
6	Critters	54
7	Bon Appetit	63
8	On My Own	69
9	Licorice Speaks	81
10	Missin' the Old Days	89
	About the Author	95

ACKNOWLEDGMENTS

The Johnstown Tribune Democrat and Editor Chip Minemyer
Johnstown Magazine and Editor Arlene Johns
Beloved fans of my newspaper column, local and nationwide
Lifelong Friends Who Shared Msgeezerette's Escapades
"Cincinnati" Cathy Miller Hagins and Family
Jere Geis
Lorraine Brinit Bush
Edith "Chipper" Valentine and Family
Jean Patterson Johnson
Sharon Howarth Layman and Family
Dick Eckman
Marlene Kough
Norman and Valerie Chynoweth
Carolyn Brumbaugh
Zachary Hubbard
Joseph Gregorchik and family
John Gregorchik
Ms. Licorice Gregorchik
Dr. Joseph Rishell and Ms. Kirby Rishell
Relatives Past and Present: Frank, Laura, Tanya, John, Nick
Extended Family: Scott, Lisa & Family, Becky V, Evans & Carney Families,
Wendy, Linda, Aunt Dolly and Ma & Pa Bender
Precious Face Book Friends
Dr. Larry Beatty and Staff
Staff and Doctors at Conemaugh Memorial Medical Center
All Church Family of former St Rochus Parish
Former Students (Alumni) of Greater Johnstown Area Vocational
Technical School and some former faculty colleagues
All employees of Giant Eagle Market, Goucher Street
Rachel Nagy and Hubert Liu, Johnstown Bishop McCort High School
students who provided expert technical assistance

Watching from above:
Ken Post
Leanne Papinchak
Johnathan Freeburg
Denise Trautman Karwoski
Chip Markel
Len Lacue.

FORWARD

JOHNSTOWN MAGAZINE article April 2017
(reprinted with permission)
Monthly feature...."Let's Meet...."

DESPITE SETBACKS, THIS WRITER SEES HUMOR IN WHATEVER LIFE HANDS HER.

JM: Have you lived in Johnstown all your life?

Yes. Mom grew up in Philadelphia and met Dad when he attended medical school there. I was born in 1949. In 1952 Dad developed TB, and was quarantined at a sanatorium for 3 years.
 Johnstown loomed new and scary for Mom alone with "little me." We spent a lot of that time in Philly with the "Grands" and in Jersey with other relatives.

JM: Tell us about your memories of old Johnstown.

Time spent in Philly made me fearless. I mastered public transportation and was allowed to ride the city bus at age 8. Times were innocent then. A kid could play and not end up on a milk carton the next day.
 My friends lived nearby. We'd meet on the bus and explore Johnstown's urban wonders. We weren't scared because there was a different attitude.
 People took pride in themselves. Men wore hats (I think there was a law) and tipped them politely to ladies. We kids offered seats to grannies on

crowded buses.

Specialty shops displayed the latest fashions. Bakeries and candy stores kept us from fitting into them. Woolworth's and Glosser's department stores smelled like roasted peanuts and adventure.

Movies entertained us on rainy days. The City Hall basement restroom was clean and safe. We'd hop off the bus and, with Morley's dog (an iconic local sculpture)to guard us, we'd dash down the cement steps to touch up lipstick or tease hair.

After all, MR. RIGHT (or MR. RIGHT-NOW) might be just across the street, gazing at drums or a shiny guitar in Weisor's Music Store's window.

JM: Did you always want to be a writer?

Actually, Cowgirl was my first career choice. Junior High introduced me to humor writers Jean Kerr, Erma Bombeck, and Jean Shepherd. I always had a gift for seeing the craziness in any situation. I wanted to write and make folks smile. My parents were appalled.

"Writers starve in attics," warned Mom.

"You need a profession," declared Dad. "Nursing, teaching, or the brasserie factory. I wasn't temperamentally suited for poverty, so I opted for teaching.

I am one of nine students who comprised the first 4 year graduating class at the University of Pittsburgh at Johnstown, April 1971.

JM: What did you like about teaching?

Everything was new. City Schools called me to "sub" the day after I graduated.

UPJ initiated a government sponsored program, "Trial by Fire." Returning Vietnam Vets, displaced housewives, and others searching for direction took 3 courses over a summer…Math, English, and History, to sharpen their college entry-level skills. What a great idea! I worked three summers until funding ran out.

1972 marked Greater Johnstown Vocational Technical School's second year of operation. They hired me.

It was an awesome concept. Educators put vocational skills, technical training, and academics under one roof. Seven districts sent students. The diversity created magic. City kids mixed with rural, jocks with nerds, future blue collars with bookworms in a city known as a melting pot of ethnicity. It delighted me to participate in such an innovative approach to learning. I was a "Spartan" for 15 years.

When financial circumstances changed some years later, I "subbed" in eight different districts for five more years.

JM: Where do your ideas come from?

Humor is everywhere. I'm handicapped but I thank God daily for medical technology and after-market replacement body parts. Some folks boast about their robust gene pools. I emerged from a septic tank.

People are reading this thinking, "How sad!" I'm sitting here laughing, recalling my first ride on one of Giant Eagles' electric shopping carts.

My elderly relatives are almost gone, but my "golden girls" and their friends had enough zany exploits to give me material for years.

I squeezed every ounce of daredevil opportunity out of my "Wonder Years," and God has mercifully allowed me to remember it all.

JM: What does your future hold?

I've begun my twelfth year of writing my column for the Trib. I have FANS! People LIKE ME. I've written a slew of columns and plan to select some of my best for a book, a collection like Dave Barry makes.

JM: Finally, are those stories ALL TRUE?

Absolutely. I saw Bruce Springsteen when I "summer-jobbed" at the Shore in 1966. I celebrated turning 65 (and Medicare eligibility) by renting the Silver Drive-In for an afternoon. A rock band rehearsed in my basement for 15 years!

My friend Joe has a Scottish terrier, Licorice, who is my protégé. I *may* stretch things a bit when Licorice substitutes for me, but she has an astounding vocabulary and humbles me when I watch her paws fly over the computer keyboard.

See, I never learned to type.

CHAPTER 1: KID STUFF

IT'S ELEMENTARY, MY DEAR

Our paper recently ran a photo of demolition progress on a building. A CVC Pharmacy would occupy that corner. But nothing registered until I saw that picture of my former grade school, Stutzman, reduced to a pile of rubble.

In 1954, Cincinnati Cathy (my best pal from age 3) and I attended Tioga St a.m. kindergarten. We learned the pledge of allegiance, not to wear a skirt on the sliding board, and never to eat paste, no matter WHO tells you it tastes good.

1st through 6th grades, we went to Stutzman, which had no cafeteria! Imagine, a school WITHOUT tater tots, peanut butter coated celery, and the epitome of "mystery meats," The Porkette.

Yes, the district bussed us 2 round trips daily: to school at 8, home for lunch at 12, back to class at 1, and home again at 4.

Imagine gassing up those busses at today's prices. Gas now costs more than beer. Perhaps we should all just park our vehicles and get loaded.

Schools aren't just rooms with blackboards, stairwells, stall bathrooms and, usually, incredibly poor heating systems. Schools hold the memories of those who filled them.

By 2nd grade, officials decided to separate Cathy and me.

Mrs. Bittorf, my 2nd grade teacher, wore herself out teaching us to read. She gloated over her "red birds;" stoically tolerated her "blue birds;" and snapped irritably at us "pigeons."

Cathy's 2nd grade teacher oozed patience. Miss Pringle looked like a Persian cat. She wore suits and blouses with ruffled collars, pinning huge brooches at her neckline every day.

No one misbehaved. She seemed so fragile, kids thought she would break.

The 3rd grade curriculum menu featured "multiplication tables." Principal James, in a disoriented moment, scheduled Cathy and me together again. Mrs. Tredennick nearly had a breakdown. Both Cathy and I remain awful at math!

Miss Horoff, my 4th grade teacher, looked exactly like Kim Novak. She sported a perfect blond French twist, impeccably manicured nails, high heels and pencil skirts.

Her appearance wasn't wasted on my "crush," a red-haired kid who rode my bus. One afternoon, he tripped over a doorstop watching Miss H stroll up the hall.

She dashed to his aid (probably the highpoint of his primary school experience). As I watched her soothe his injured neck with those perfect fingers, I vowed never to bite my nails again.

Mrs. Dodd taught 6th grade, and played the piano, an old Spinet upright.

I've watched movies with Army drill sergeants who weren't as tough as Mrs. Dodd (Ever see an Officer and a Gentleman? She could've taken Lou Gossett in 30 seconds, tops!).

When you're prepubescent, you're reluctant to sing in public (or anywhere else).

If Mrs. Dodd said, "SING!" baby, you SANG!

MOVIES BENEATH THE STARS

When spring arrives, I catch drive-in movie fever.
In our area, we enjoy 3 outdoor theaters in a thirty mile radius. Movies beneath the stars seem, well... heavenly.

Our shopping plaza started out in the fifties as a drive-in.

Back then, drive-ins were open seven nights a week. Mom always knew which picture was playing. She, Aunt Ethel, and I saw every new feature.

For kids, drive-ins meant endless fun. The playground beckoned with a push-style merry-go-round and giant swings. The snack bar tempted us with candy and popcorn.

Preparing for a drive-in jaunt smacked of packing for a safari. Mom brought a blanket, bed pillow, my pajamas, soda for me, and a thermos of coffee to share with Ethel.

Kids scrambled from the playground when the cartoon flashed on the big screen. Bugs and Mickey mesmerized me, but by the time the first movie started, I'd be stifling yawns.

Mom would make a tent out of the blanket, my "dressing room" where I'd don my jammies. Songs by Sinatra or Fred Astaire's tapping would lull me to sleep, nestled in the back of Mom's Plymouth Savoy.

Grown-ups counted on kids zoning out since adult subjects usually dominated the second film.

But I saw stuff! Occasionally I'd awaken and catch snippets of some very mature flicks. I watched "The Bridge on the River Kwai" explode, and saw Shirley MacLaine get shot in "Some Came Running." But it didn't bother me because, even at 8, I understood that movies were make-believe.

One summer night, I had a sleep-over at my friend Jere's house. Her older sister Nancy's boyfriend arrived to take her to the drive-in.

Don, the BF, drove a Nash Metropolitan (Think 1950's Mini-Cooper but without the phenomenal gas mileage).

Our brains hatched a plan. We'd stowaway on the floor in the back. When things got romantic, we'd pop up, demanding goodies in exchange for our silence.

The backseat of a Metropolitan consisted of a vinyl-covered plank with almost no leg room. An adult would fit if he tucked his knees in his ears. Two elves could sit comfortably. That night, two 9 year old extortionists crouched in the darkness.

Don put his arm around Nancy, but their first kiss sparked a giggle fit that gave us away.

They bought us off with Hershey Bars, then drove our naughty little keisters straight home.

By then, Jere's mom missed us and was searching frantically. We caught the dickens for our prank, but we declared the adventure totally worth it.

PEEPS IN PERIL

Animals fascinated my mom. Riding the train between Johnstown and Philly, she saw horses, pigs, sheep, cows....a "Mattel See-and-Say" of farm critters.

When I turned 5, my dad got a cat. He named her "Miss Kitty" after Marshall Dillon's dance hall gal on GUNSMOKE.

Miss Kitty, a demolitions specialist, prowled the kitchen counters and clawed the club chairs to shreds. The day she climbed the Christmas tree, breaking dozens of glass, heirloom ornaments, her time ran out.

My dad had a patient with a farm (Yes, in the 50's and 60's doctors still made house calls!). Miss Kitty assumed her new job of barn supervisor. She ran a tight yard.

I'd visit, and she'd cuddle and purr for a few minutes, but quickly resumed walking her beat. I had nothing against farm animals except the aroma. As for chickens, you couldn't pet them, walk them, or play ball with them. Or BATH them!

In 1956, my dad developed TB. He was hospitalized at a special sanitarium during the next two years. Mom's sister, Ethel, a widow, moved in with us.

One morning, a stray dog turned up on our stoop. Looking exactly like "Tramp" from the Disney movie, this short-haired gray mutt was playful, streetwise, and protective. He understood the "house-broken" concept, more or less, and if a chipmunk sneezed, he barked ferociously. "Tinker" became our guard dog.

In 1957, Grant's Department Store fronted on Main St. It had a smaller back door. "Seasonal items" were displayed in that rear area so Christmas trees, inflatable plastic swimming pools, and other bulky stuff could be purchased and loaded easily.

Easter baskets, plastic-wrapped chocolate bunnies, and 5 lb jars of jelly beans were clunky. But, displayed along with these Easter necessities were…peeps. These tiny, noisy, helpless, not-quite-a-chick yet creatures came dyed in ghastly colors…taxi cab yellow, grass green, hot pink and vivid purple.

Mom brought two "taxis" home in a shoe box on the city bus.

"Dorothy, what's wrong with you?" Ethel scolded.

Tinker sniffed the newcomers and then ignored them. He probably didn't like how they smelled any more than I did.

Apparently, they came with instructions: "sod in box bottom, include water, keep warm." Mom placed the box on the floor in the dining room, just under a wall outlet. In our "junk drawer,' she found a 60 watt bulb that would plug directly into a socket.

Easter morning, we woke up to a smell that permeated the house. Tinker dashed down the steps, but abruptly halted about a foot from the crime scene. Tinker KNEW that smell!

He crept backwards, looking at me as if to say, "I promise, I'll NEVER pee on the carpet again!"

Mom cried a little and Ethel stashed the corpses in a vacant field down the street.

Dad returned the following spring. To celebrate, Mom happily marched into the house with another shoe box. Purple peeps (there seems to be a song there…).

My dad removed 60 watt bulbs from her reach, thus preventing this Buster Brown shoe box from becoming another Easy Bake Oven. Tinker shrugged.

Easter morning found us all happy, healthy, and safe. Mom must have studied, because those freaky critters thrived. By Father's Day, they resided in the garage, having outgrown 5 other boxes. Each weighed about 4 lbs.

The final "Colonel Sanders" battle was classic.

Dorothy, they're going to get bigger." You could hear the purple feathers flapping.

"I'll drive them to the bus stop and give each one a token," Dad growled.

In the end, we took them to Miss Kitty's farm. The cat looked astonished when 2 purple chickens bounded out of Dad's Pontiac. Amazed cows, sheep, pigs, and horses muttered.

But the ROOSTER! Poor "Foghorn Leghorn!"

"Ah say, ah say....what? WHAT?"

SOCK IT TO ME

"Very well done, children," angelic Sister Beatrice smiled at the gaggle of 9 and 10 year old faces in the classroom. "We'll see you next Saturday at 10."

The sound of a rubber band snapping angrily caught our attention. Sister Mary Rambo, the pit bull of Christianity, waved her Missal menacingly. "Be prompt." she snarled.

Welcome to First Communion prep Catechism, just where 10 year old me wanted to spend 6 early spring Saturday mornings.

City wide, each Catholic church had only 2 or 3 pre-communicants each year. Practical economics brought kids from churches I'd never heard of, many of which were rich and strict in customs and traditions.

Our St. Rochus boys wore suits and girls wore time-honored white dresses and veils.

Some gals had gown-like dresses that passed through generations. Every year, some loving granny stitched a new bow or embroidered a flower to mark the frock's passage.

G-Pa Mikesic died at least 15 year before my birth. He and his cousin immigrated to New York at 15, traveling light. No chance of an heirloom dress there.

Mom and I rode the bus downtown to Penney's, Communion chic headquarters, and the site of the first of many fierce knee socks vs hosiery battles.

Mom and I fought over every item I wore from the day I left the playpen. She, of course, selected my dress. I gave in pretty quickly about the dorky veil because secretly, I thought it was kinda cool. Then, she bought me a new pair of white, 100% cotton knee socks.

Weeks before, I pedaled to Woolworth's and purchased nylons for 39 cents. Determined, I stashed them at home.

Every class has a wise guy. Ours, Freddie, mean as a snake, slithered to his desk weekly and plotted his disruptions. He had attitude and imagination, plus anger and probably undiagnosed ADHD. He spent enough time in the corner to caulk every stained glass window in the building.

I lost the sock battle and, on C Day, I grumbled the whole way down the road, vowing never to speak to Mom again.

The service began, and I noticed twin boys who came from one of those mysterious, rigid churches new to me. "Notice" doesn't TOUCH IT.

They wore white satin DRESSES! Lace ruffles adorned the high necks, and the skirts were balloon-style, yards of fabric gathered with elastic just below the knees.

Apparently, unisex ruled at ground-breaking "Our Lady of Unimaginable Misery."

Oh, and did I mention the headgear? Adding insult to injury, both sported daisy garlands with white ribbon streamers.

They stoically endured the ceremony. Freddie nearly burst an artery trying to control himself, knowing that Sister Mary Rambo would gut him like a fish if he misbehaved.

But he made faces, and noises. The brothers ground their teeth while smoke billowed out their ears.

And, as the bells chimed, a miracle occurred. My J. C. Penney knee socks didn't seem so bad. I prayed that when Mass ended, the twins would ditch their sacred garments, chase Freddie down the river wall and beat the wafer out of him.

We got into the car, and, wordlessly, I hugged my mother.

The next day, I Schwinned back to Woolworth's where I returned the hose, intact, still in the wrapper, and received my 39 cent refund.

SALUTING LUNCH LADIES

My friend, Barb, a truly outstanding mother, works as a "Lunch Lady" at her children's school. She can keep an eye on her young'uns without being a "hover-mother."

My mom became a lunch lady in Sept 1967, the same day I began college classes. She started at the bottom as a "tray-scraper." However, in less than a month, the administration realized that Mom was an amazing, untapped natural resource.

My mom could scream. If hollering was an Olympic event, she'd have been a gold medalist. Think nails scratching a blackboard are blood-curdling? Mom's shrill, ear-splitting shrieks could peel paint off a wall!

The brass heard her banshee howls when food fights broke out, or if some little snot tried to smuggle his fork into the discard tray.

They promoted her immediately, giving her a whistle and stationing her on the playground, a force to be reckoned with. Any child pushing, kicking, or otherwise clobbering classmates felt Dorothy's wrath when she grabbed that whistle and roared.

Doris Day starred in a 1960 movie based on a Jean Kerr novel, "Please Don't Eat the Daisies." The film addressed issues of child-rearing, gender roles, and pet care. By today's standards, it was ethically and politically incorrect in countless ways.

In 50's and 60's movies, folks who seemed otherwise normal would frequently burst into song.

Doris played a mom who volunteered as an after-school playground monitor. She sings 3 or 4 songs including her signature tune, "Que Sera Sera."

At one point, she strums a ukulele and shepherds the kiddies as they dance around a Maypole chirping a number called (ready?) "Please Don't eat the Daisies."

Watching Doris police the swing set zone reminds me of Mom, who spent 5 school years terrorizing grade school miscreants.

Mercifully, Mom never whipped out a uke and trilled any melodies. But I guarantee you that, between 1967 and 1972, no one ever ate a daisy at Southmont Elementary.

Have a nice day, Barb!

OFFICER HAPPY, DEBONAIRE MAN ABOUT TOWN

What a special day! It's Mothers' Day and National Law Enforcement Week begins today.

My mom did not get the child she wanted. From the day I left my playpen, Mom and I battled over everything: food, clothes, grades, curfews, boys – you name it.

Mothers and police share common concerns.
God bless the mothers who put up with little brats like me.

God Bless the blue lives who protect, serve, and sacrifice to keep us safe.

Imagine facing unknown danger daily. Crooks, sociopaths, and murderers lack consciences. Laws mean nothing. Officers are expected to pursue criminals in a climate of social unrest, distrust, and moral defiance.

Readers are wondering, "How can she blend these topics and make us laugh?" Work with me.

Johnstown PA's history distinguishes us. Reminders of our heritage like The Inclined Plane and our could-be-magnificent again (with some TLC) railroad station have endured. Morley's dog, a popular statue from bygone days, now barks all over town.

Other local icons were products of their time frames, not meant to last. Yet, when someone mentions one, folks light up.

The bell atop Joe Johns Junior High, an antique Wise Potato Chip billboard by an old diner, our local stadium's upper deck ("Peanut Heaven") and the Happy Policeman are fondly etched in our memories.

Legend tells that Coca Cola donated a half-dozen smiling metal crossing guards to our area, strategically placed to alert motorists approaching school zones.

A rural gal recalled one near her bus stop. Others reported Officer Happys guarding city schools.

One fella admitted to assisting "cop-napper" buddies in stuffing one in the trunk of an Oldsmobile in the late 50's. Because of the tight fit, he huddled in the trunk with the "victim."

I know, personally, that another stood on a Napoleon Street safety island protecting Johnstown High students.

The Happy Policeman was clearly a "man about town."

Back to mothers.

Few Philadelphians drove cars. Mass transit (buses, commuter trains, the subway) handled citizen travel.

Dad taught Mom, a Philly gal, to drive. On a good day, her skill was marginal. She loathed "Easy Grade," a hilly road winding to downtown. To avoid it, we'd cruise to the Incline and let the cable cars haul her '53 Plymouth up and down.

Our local War Memorial arena offered daytime parking. It was also closest to the Incline ramp. We'd leave the Savoy and walk across town. Despite several fender-benders in the parking lot, Mom persevered.

Then one day, the Incline was closed for maintenance. With white knuckles clutching the steering wheel, she descended "Easy Everest" slowly and safely.

Errands run, we turned right onto the street leading to the hillside road for the first time, ever. Mom spotted the island and "Officer About-to-be-Unhappy."

"Where should I go?" she gasped.

I shut my eyes, feeling the car bounce as it jumped the island. I could hear Officer Happy crunching under the heavy V-8.

Real policemen helped us exit the Plymouth because, while the front end rested on the 10 inch curb, the rear wheels remained on the street.

A tow truck with a winch arrived, but they had to remove Happy's carcass from the huge chrome grill before they could hook the cable.

Moral of the story: Even metal policemen confront danger. And mothers? Ya gotta love 'em.

CHAPTER 2: ADOLESCENT ANTICS

DANCING WITH DIMPS

A TV ad for an online shoe outlet made me "twist" in my chair.

"Let's Dance," a lively 60's tune, played as attractive young couples gyrated in "mod" attire. The guys wore loud plaid Robert Hall jackets and gaudy ties. Gals with bouffant hairdos balanced on platform shoes with 4 inch heels, reinforcing a theory I totally believe: Cinderella proved a point; the right footwear can change your life!

From the day my friends and I discovered teen dances at the Grove, we were hooked. Neither snow nor rain could keep us from strutting our limited junior high stuff at these Friday night events.

The Grove, a large gym, blasted pop music on a 45 rpm record player. We learned all the trendy dances. We "mashed potatoes," "cha-cha-ed," and "watusi-ed."

Girls performed the intricate steps. The boys watched.

Janice Ian sang," I learned the truth at 17, that love is just for beauty queens...."

Janice didn't quite get it.

There are pretty girls, of course, and there are "dimps." Dimps usually have fine qualities: clever wit, generosity, radiant personalities, but average looks.

14 year old boys felt entitled to Farrahs, Annettes, Twiggies, or majorettes.

Pretties hang out with dimps because it makes them look even prettier. Dimps understood the law of "supply and demand" and counted on "overflow."

Plus, no female ever visits a ladies' room alone, so dimps solved that dilemma as well.

Girls travel in packs, much like wolves. I was blessed to belong to an eye-catching, diverse group.

Lorraine, an enchanting, graceful brunette, could cha-cha tirelessly.

"Hornerstown Cathy" (now "Cincinnati Cathy") an athletic platinum blond, mastered the tricky dance steps. She "mashed potatoes" and "watusi-ed" with abandon.

Chipper, our ingénue (think Sandra Dee), had 1000 watt eyes and an effervescence that out-bubbled Alka Seltzer. She stopped the show when she danced to "Wipeout."

As a dancer, I was a "limp" dimp. When I tried the "Bristol Stomp," I looked like a clumsy forest ranger grinding out campfire embers.

Since we needed a parent chauffeur, we started begging and pleading on Thursdays.

Cathy's dad had a tiny green Studebaker. We arrived safely if we all breathed in rhythm.

Chipper's dad drove a non-descript Plymouth.

My mom's Ford ranch wagon rode like a wheel barrow.

But Lorraine's dad's Chrysler Imperial guaranteed we'd arrive stylishly.

Maybe 5 slow songs spun per evening. The stag line rarely moved. Dimps and wallflowers gleaned satisfaction watching pretties being trampled and groped.

Bright lights flashed on at 11, and we scrambled for purses and jackets.

Heading home, we whispered and giggled and dreamed of the next Friday night, and the one after that.

After all, a prince on a white horse holding a glass slipper should be easy to spot in a room full of t-shirt clad, acne-faced losers.

Hope springs eternal.

SUMMER JOB BLUES

My first ever summer job lasted exactly two and one half hours.

I was hired at a soft-serve ice cream stand at a local park. In 1964, cones with curls on top ruled.

You could only practice when you had a customer. The product couldn't be dumped back into the machine.

I couldn't twirl that stuff to save my life. I disgraced my paper hat; started at noon, fired at 2:30.

Back then, everyone sought summer jobs.

My friend Becky already had her license. She drove her mom's car to a huge theme park Thursdays through Sundays to enchant children as Little Miss Muffet. On sizzling days she nearly melted into a puddle of storybook ooze wearing her heavy costume.

But the job had perks. That summer, she dated the dashing captain of the Good Ship Lollipop.

Hornerstown Cathy took a waitressing job at a family-owned restaurant. Her supervisor was the owner's grouchy daughter.

One night, Cathy put the giant vat of Hershey Syrup on a shelf without tightening the lid. The next morning "Grouchette," reaching for it, became a human fudgesicle.

Luckily, Cathy didn't get fired.

Scrambling to find other employment after Curly Q, I landed at Fun City. Located 3 miles out of town, it featured a huge swimming pool and six-ride amusement park, attracting kids of all ages.

The "swim gate" was the best spot to work. You could check out every person who arrived and, most importantly, the boys!

I usually wound up in the ride ticket booth, selling 10 cent tickets to frazzled parents and whiny little kids. The job paid 50 cents an hour. If your cash drawer didn't jive with the numbered tickets on the roll, the boss docked your pay.

After losing 75 cents once and 35 cents another time, I quickly mastered change-making!

That skill has served me well.

Now, 44 years later, I've come full-circle. I sit in a booth selling 10 cent tickets again, this time for my church's summer festivals.

For the most part, I love my customers. But I recall exceptions.

An irate man demanded his $1.20 back when the grill ran out of hot dogs. Each 10 cent ticket is clearly marked "No Refunds." I suggested that he sell them to the lady in line behind him, but he belligerently refused.

With a dozen impatient folks waiting, I reluctantly gave him the cash. Then I reached under my counter and grabbed the super-soaker squirt gun I'd brought along.

As he turned to leave, I took my shot. I nailed him square in the back of the head, then stashed my weapon.

The other customers squealed gleefully as he looked around for the source of the "cloudburst."

"Will you get in trouble for that?" laughed the next man in line.

"Nah," I assured him. "Besides, I used holy water!"

BEAUTY AND THE BEACH

I love the beach.

The summer I turned fourteen, my family took an ocean vacation. We included my friend Cathy. My aunt and uncle owned a house in picturesque Stone Harbor, New Jersey, where we spent two unforgettable weeks.

Cathy and I vowed to return. In 1966, after months of begging and cajoling, our folks allowed us to set out ON OUR OWN for a seashore summer. We were seventeen.

Conditions applied, of course. We had to stay in Stone Harbor. We had to work and save money for our senior year that lay ahead. Pictures, prom and graduation didn't come cheap.

Toting two heavy suitcases each, we rode the train to Philly and connected with the Shore Train. My uncle met us at Cape May and drove us to our accommodations, a rambling old rooming house, "The Carolyn".

It featured a WOODEN fire escape. Fellow tenants included families and other summer job seekers, mostly college age.

Employment opportunities abounded. Cathy's waitress job had rotating shifts so she could still enjoy the beach.

I settled for two part-time spots. Mornings I worked at Barton's Bakery. Alternate afternoons and evenings, I stocked shelves at the 5 & 10.

My job at the bakery instilled in me a lasting hatred of all pastry. I loathe "stickiness." Donut glaze has a half-life like uranium. To this day, I detest cake, pie, cookies, etc.

In addition to being a baker, Mr. Barton was a bookie. Strange characters bellied up to our counter each morning. We never knew if they wanted brownies or the daily double at Atlantic City Race Track.

One late July morning, I reported to work to find only smoldering rubble. The bakery burned down overnight.

No one knew if the giant ovens malfunctioned or if Mr. B ticked somebody off.

I walked back to The Carolyn dejectedly.

Our next-room neighbor sat on the porch swing. Amanda had a fabulous summer job. Twenty-one and about to start her senior year at Penn State, she worked as a go-go girl.

Go-go was wholesome then. "Shindig" and "Hullabaloo" were popular TV staples.

I plunked down on the swing beside her.

"What's wrong?" Amanda asked.

"Barton's burned down. I'm out of a job," I sighed.

"Maybe you could work with us," she suggested. "Two girls quit last week."

"Dancing? ME?"

"Why not?" she grinned. "It's good money and they pay cash."

I knew Amanda thought I was eighteen or older. I also knew that, to stay until Labor Day, I needed a second job. I gathered my courage.

"I'll do it!"

At my first gig, the Grand Opening of a Firestone Tire Center, four of us danced on the back of a flat bed trailer. I launched my month-long career in a borrowed dress and boots, gyrating to Martha and The Vandellas' "Dancin' In The Street."

How appropriate was THAT?

SEASIDE SUMMER NIGHTS

As a columnist, I frequently ask readers to share opinions on various subjects. In 2007, Readers voted for their favorite classic rock tune.

Friends of mine have a band that was scheduled to play a benefit concert at our local bandshell. They were delighted to help.

Bruce Springstein's "Born To Run" was performed to an enthusiastic crowd on a perfect September Sunday afternoon.

The week before, a female contestant on TV's "Millionaire" reminisced to the host about a fabulous "garage band" that played for high school in her native New Jersey.

Who was the lead singer of that fledgling group? Our Bruce!

"Did he display star quality even then?" the host asked.

"Absolutely!" the lady drooled.

In 1966, "Cincinnati Cathy" (Hornerstown Cathy then) and I spent our 17th summer on our own in Stone Harbor, N.J.

Seeking seasonal jobs, we stayed in a cheap, ramshackle boarding house with other summer workers and families on budgets.

One afternoon on the beach, Cathy encountered Hal, a Stone Harbor "townie."

"There's a really cool band playing tonight at a bar in Avalon," he told her. "Would you like to go hear them?"

"Could we double?" she asked. "I'd like my roommate to go, too."

"Sure," Hal agreed. "I'll bring my uncle. He's a lifeguard. We'll pick you up at 8."

"His UNCLE?" I howled when Cathy told me. I get stuck with some fossil?"

"Uncle Lifeguard" was 19. Hal was 18. Family ties!

In 1966, New Jersey had no auto inspection. If a vehicle had four wheels and a motor, you could drive it.

At 8 that evening, Hal and uncle Lifeguard rolled up in a 1951 Pontiac Starfire – with a split windshield.

Perfect gentlemen, they opened the doors for us and we hopped in to discover…folding chairs! The car's interior had been gutted. The only seat bolted to the frame was half the front bench on the driver's side. "I'm restoring it!" Hal announced proudly.

Did you ever sit on a folding chair in a moving car? You'd remember if you had. Mercifully, our destination sat only two flat miles down the road.

Back then, the drinking age in Jersey was 18, making the state a Mecca for partiers None of us had any interest in alcohol. We craved only the music. Even without direct supervision, we behaved.

The awesome band totally blew our minds. We danced the night away.

"These guys rock!" I commented to Uncle Lifeguard. "Who are they?"

" Don't know the name," Unc replied, "but I hear they came from Asbury Park. And that lead singer? Someone said his name was Bruce."

DATIN' AT THE DRIVE-IN

At 18, I had mt first drive-in movie date. I sat in the front seat of a blue Ford Fairlane
 watching a bizarre biker flick, "Born Losers." I remember the guy, the car, and the movie because that was my first step toward teen-aged independence..

Twenty years ago, I contacted an excellent local artist and asked him to paint that first date for me. We met at Denny's, where I roughed out a sketch on the back of a placemat. It shows our Silver Drive-In marquee, the screen, cars and speakers and, across the street, our old Tops Diner.

All great Silver dates ended with fries 'n gravy at Tops.

In 1968, the summer movie to see was Franco Zeffirelli's "Romeo and Juliet." The controversial Italian director had cast 15 year-olds in the leads. Word on the street declared the picture hot and steamy, ideal drive-in fare.

I saw it with a guy named Bob. His pal Fred and his date came along. Half an hour into the thing, Fred tapped me on the shoulder. "You go to college, Michele. You know stuff. What language are those people speaking?"

Nearly speechless, I finally answered, "English, Fred. Your native tongue."

1970's "Airport" featured Dean Martin piloting a damaged 747 to Burt Lancaster's snowbound airport. Suspense, action, and subplots glued me to the edge of my seat. Incredibly, my date that evening, Tony, fell asleep.

When the movie ended, I shook him and we drove home.

When it came to drive-in dates, the most memorable happened in my friend Dick's hearse! Dick worked in Maryland and came home weekends.

He'd purchased an old hearse he'd found somewhere down south.

He'd come to fetch me in his car, so my parents never knew about it. They would have chained me in the basement before they let me go cruisin' in a hearse!

We'd pull into a slot at the drive-in, and the row would empty almost immediately. People freaked out at the sight and moved elsewhere!

Sometimes Dick parked horizontally. Speakers in both the front and back created primitive "surround sound." We'd sit cross-legged and watch the picture through the huge side window (he'd remove the drape, of course!).

Horror movies dominated the late '60's and early '70's. "Night of the Living Dead," "Dracula," and ANYTHING starring Vincent Price filled outdoor theaters.

At the scariest moments, Dick would fire up the hearse, put the parking lights on, and cruise slowly between the rows of vehicles. We had a blast!

I still treasure the drive-in.

I'm no teenager any more, but Hollywood under the stars still creates magic for me.

FLEXING MY MUSCLES

In spring, a man's fancy turns to…AUTOMOBILES! NASCAR, Muscle cars, antiques, dragsters.

'60's and '70's trends usually caught on late here…NOT so with cars. The Beach Boys sang "Shut Down;" Ronny and the Daytona's sang "G. T. O." "Drag City" by Jan and Dean, and Wilson Pickett's "Mustang Sally" swept across the nation.

Youthful boomer males expected autos to reach benchmarks set by muscle cars. These phenomenal machines offered hi-performance V-8 engines. Shiny chrome, maybe a spoiler, and eye-catching custom wheels completed the macho vehicle dream .

I learned to drive in my mom's '63 Mustang, yellow with wire spoke hubcaps. I scrubbed the interior and detailed the dash every month, hoping someday Lemonade would be mine.

Philadelphia folks use public transportation. Johnstowners drive. My dad, a confirmed car zealot, believed in bigger, better, newer, faster. He bought Mom a silver Olds convertible and taught her to drive.

She hated the Olds; she hated driving; and Dad's approval ratings weren't very high either.

Mom preferred plain, ugly, utilitarian crates with few or no amenities. She drove dealerships crazy by demanding "NO RADIOS !" I thought her Ford Ranch Wagon was drab until I saw her '84 4-cylinder Escort (We named it "GRUNT").

Meanwhile, I "cruised the strip" in Lemonade. At Stuver's, a local burger hang out, I met Roger, a Roy Orbison look-alike who drove an Olds

442 named "Disturbance."

Another friend, Dave, operated a garage. His every-day ride was an International Scout with more lights than the Times Square Christmas tree. However, each summer Sunday, he loaded "Quicksilver" on his trailer; a '55 (Just-for-racing) Chevy Bel Air that won widespread acclaim at area drag strips.

The cars mesmerized me. And I AM my father's daughter. I hatched a scheme.

With graduation 2 weeks away, I announced, "I decided to go to Wellsley."

My Mom glowed...an IVY girl. My dad, thinking expenses, nearly burst an artery.

Now, I wanted to attend Wellsley as much as a raccoon wants to be baptized. When Dad suggested a tour of the newly built University of Pittsburgh Johnstown Campus, we spent a Sunday afternoon there.

"This is beautiful!" Dad exclaimed. "And you would be a member of the first 4-year class to graduate in Johnstown."

I nodded. I hadn't thought about that perk, and the campus was awesome.

"Reasonable tuition," he pointed out. "No food or dorm expenses if you live at home. We'd get you a reliable car for commuting."

Mission accomplished! My dad (fan of bigger, better, faster, newer) would choose a car for me.

A lime-gold '67 Mustang appeared in the driveway, and I drove it proudly and happily until, after 3 years, the brakes failed rolling down a steep street. I steered into someone's bumpy yard to stop.

Meanwhile, my folks locked horns again over a MOM-mobile. Spontaneously, she traded Lemonade for a beautiful, burnt orange, 6 cylinder Plymouth Barracuda with snow white interior. She didn't "test drive." She said it made her look pretty.

She looked pretty, but couldn't drive it. No power steering.

Dad approached me. "I'd like to trade your Mustang on a car for your mother. *I WILL PICK THIS ONE* ! We'll hand the Barracuda down to you."

From Ford "pony world," I entered Mopar Glamour Land. The "Fish" attracted attention everywhere.

Dad arrived with Mom's new ride...a vile, vomit-green Plymouth Duster with, of course, power steering, and a trunk capable of hauling a rhinoceros.

Mom handed me the Duster keys one evening. "Sears is having a paint sale. Get me 6 gallons of 'eggshell'. Take the Duster. That carton would never fit in your tiny trunk."

Of course, I stopped at Stuver's.

The Duster drew a crowd. Neither my dad nor I knew that the car had a 340 small block, the most potent engine ever available! A genuine screamer, it arrogantly kicked sand into the grills of the big blocks, just because it could!

This legendary motor awakened racing fantasies in every guy!

All summer, I made up fibs explaining why I needed to borrow the Duster. Sharon had boxes for Goodwill; her cousin bought a hope chest; the Mr. Turtle pool we bought for Betty's nephew wouldn't fit in her Nova.

No Goodwill, no chest, no Mr. Turtle – I was on a quarter-mile bridge span, part of our local expressway, racing. That stretch of highway was usually deserted after dark.

I beat a 390 Cougar; left a '69 GTO in the dust; and blew the doors off an SS396 Chevelle. The night I raced a '70 Mustang 302, I hit a skunk.

My Mom exploded. "Is Goodwill repairing skunks?" I was forbidden to touch the Duster ever again.

But I had more muscle to flex. In '73, I started "super saving." I bought generic groceries, cut my own grass, and shoveled my snowy driveway. I rented out a room in my 2 bedroom house to a college girl.

April 14, 1977, I purchased a '74 red Corvette t-top for $5G. I sold it for $15G 20 years later.

I had the best of 3 worlds, some quite by accident. But I wouldn't trade a minute. OK, *maybe* the skunk.

CRUISIN' AND CLUNKIN'

Memorial Day displays summer's bounty: Flowers, lawn furniture, flip-flops, grills, fire flies, graduations, romance.

"In the spring, a young man's fancy lightly turns to thoughts of love." Alfred Lord Tennyson.

"Spring is when the SAP starts to run." Aunt Sis.

"Are you going out wearing THAT?" Mom.

Both Alice Cooper and Steely Dan wrote songs exploring 19, the age that nurtures wishes, hopes and dreams, but leaves teens confused, doubtful, and pressured. You race to find your identity, but mostly you make yourself nuts.

Tennyson's young men devote one season to hormonal pursuit. Girls devote lives.

I met my precious friend Sharon at the college entrance exams. We thought alike; we finished each other's sentences. We spent summers cruising Route 56 in my Mustang.

In 1968, Route 56 had everything: Gee Bee, a discount department store; Dunkin' Donuts; the bowling alley; an ice cream parlor; and a Robert Hall's. Most of all, it featured the epitome of teen mating destinations: Stuvers Drive-Thru Diner.

Stuvers sold reasonably priced burgers, fries, chicken and shakes, but it was (paraphrasing Connie Francis) "Where the Boys Were." Guys displayed their cars, sipped soda pop, discussed carburetors, and subtly checked the girls out.

At dinner one evening, my father gave me a mission. "Pick up your Aunt Sis and her dog. They have an appointment at the vet's office downtown.

Sis, feisty and entertaining, smoked unfiltered Pall Malls. She lived in a mobile home 20 miles away. Tish, her cocker spaniel, had digestive issues and desperately needed Beano.

An idea hatched. I'd fetch Sharon, zip 20 miles, get Sis and Tish, do the appointment, and zoom them back home.

We could be 'tom-cattin' at Stuver's by 9.

The trip to the vet took 25 minutes at 75 mph. Open windows and a southern breeze kept the nitrogen, methane and nicotine fumes minimal.

Returning to the trailer park pointed us downwind. Sis filled the car with a blue nicotine haze. Tish, indignant about her immunization, emitted nitro and methane that hung in Sis's cloud.

I sped up to 80. A state trooper on the shoulder pulled behind me.

"#!$&" I snarled.

"Nice young ladies don't say THAT word," chided Sis.

Sharon and I rolled our eyes through the dense blue fog.

"I'm gonna get us out of this," I said. I took my foot off the gas and coasted. The trooper almost rear-ended me. Acting oblivious, I punched it! He lit up and pulled next to me.

NOW, I noticed him. "Mister, please stop!" I shouted. He looked amazed.

I met him at my headlight. "Officer," I blubbered, "I have a clunk! I tried going real fast and then real slow, but it still clunks." By now, I had worked up some tears.

"Calm down. Now, let's have a look." He popped the hood.

"What's wrong? Why'd we stop?" Sis asked through the smog.

"Maybe the policeman heard Michele say '#!$&'," Sharon answered.

"Where are you going?" the trooper asked, clutching a dipstick.

"Driving my aunt home," I answered innocently.

"Get in and start it up," he instructed.

I turned the key. The engine purred. "You FIXED it! " I shrieked in delight. "Sharon! No more clunk!"

"No clunk," Sharon agreed.

Baffled, he shut the hood. "Listen. I didn't do anything."

"You FIXED it," I insisted. "Thank you so much."

"I really didn't. Suppose I follow you, be sure you don't break down."

"No, you've done so much already!"

He pulled off at the next exit and waved good-bye.

Nothing magical happened at Stuver's that night. There would be similar summer nights…stupid, foolish, but glorious, because the dawn of a new era stirred us. It was an era of adventure, discovery, and freedom.

As we drove home, we laughed , compared notes, and planned for the next night, and the one after that.

CHAPTER 3: MEET THE FOLKS

AGE IS RELATIVE

Folks call certain birthdays "milestones."

"I don't believe you're gonna tell your age!" exclaimed galpal Lorraine on the eve of my 56th year.

I sorta can't believe it either. I come from a long line of liars.

My mom claimed her Social Security benefit three years late because she'd fibbed about her age. When my great aunt Bessie died, no one actually knew how old she was.

At 56 plus 1 day, I drove off one lovely spring morn to get my new photo drivers license. I opened the sun roof, plugged the Beach Boys "Endless Summer" CD in, and cruised to the DMV license center.

The place never changed. It looked the same as when I took my test there in 1965. Two nervous teens awaited their turns at the course. Inside the building, the linoleum and walls were the same. But of course, the technology had improved. I got in and out in a jiffy.

As I climbed in my car, I thought, "Four years till I come again." Then it hit me. Yikes! I'd be 60!

Fast forward to "Milestone 60." My friend Joe accompanied me to the DMV. I filled out the forms, posed for my photo, handed the old license over to be voided and received the new one.

Back in the car, I scrutinized the two pictures. "You know, I like the old photo better."

Joe smiled. "Trust me. In four years, you'll like THIS one."

I handled it this pretty well, although I swore the next person who said, "Sixty is the new fifty," would get smacked upside the head.

Another buddy of mine, Jonathan, recently freaked out when he became a great uncle at 53.

When my grandmother in Philadelphia died in 1968, the funeral home sent a car and driver to fetch her sister, the aforementioned Aunt Bessie, from New Jersey.

I greeted her in the receiving room.

"Michele, do me a favor." Bessie handed me a $1 bill. "A nice young man, really good-looking, drove me in from Mount Holly. He should be outside. Give him this tip for me."

"Sure," I obliged.

Hmm. Go to the parking lot and find a handsome young guy? My 19 year old hormones surged.

His back was to me as I approached him. "Excuse me," I began, "did you just drive an elderly woman in from Jersey?"

The man turned. He had to have been seventy!

Age is truly relative.

OH, FUDGE

Thanksgiving! Hey! Bring a dessert," they said.

I had married into a family of superb cooks. No, beyond superb; far beyond superb. One sister baked wedding cakes as a sideline; the other dips her own chocolates every Christmas. My mother-in-law baked gobs that people still fondly remember, even though she died in 19.

Then there's me, but I come by my lack of kitchen skills genetically.

My maternal grandmother was probably the worst cook in the western hemisphere. Her "dippy eggs" gave me nightmares. My dad, a doctor, would not eat at her house. My Aunt Ethel once served a Thanksgiving turkey she had roasted for only three hours.

My mom's holiday specialty, a sort of mutant brown bread fruitcake, was absolutely frightening.

"Aunt Sis" swam on my dad's side of the gene pool. She learned to cook helping in the kitchen of her parents' hotel, serving huge, heavy, ethnic meals to ravenous steelworkers. The trouble with Aunt Sis's cooking was, seventy-two hours later, you were hungry again.

Determined to prove myself worthy of the excellent culinary tradition I had married into, I started preparing that Thanksgiving dessert. An ad in the Sunday Parade Magazine convinced me to tackle "Easy-fix Peanut Butter Fudge." PARADE wouldn't lie, right?

The first problem was sugar. Half a cup short, I peered out the window of my warm kitchen at wet snow plopping into the backyard.

Should I brave the elements to run next door, or over to the market?

"Nah, who'll miss a half cup?" I rationalized, unaware that sugar provides a vital "clotting" agent in fudge.

Several steps later, the recipe instructed me to add two teaspoons of vanilla extract. I blithely tossed 2 teaspoons into the saucepan.

Then, I looked up. The brown vanilla extract bottle was STILL on the spice shelf above the range. What brown-bottled ingredient had I mistakenly added?

Gravy Master!

As you read this, years later, that fudge remains a mysterious, quivering, pulsating mass. Ever see the old horror movie classic, "The Blob"? Somewhere, on a landfill, that fudge is still moving. For dessert, I brought a package of Oreos.

JULIE'S AULD LANG SYNE

C'mon, time travel with me to 1958. We're standing on Chandler Ave in front of Milan's Café.

There's my dad, wearing his wide-brimmed hat, trousers yanked up to his armpits, and a sport jacket. All men wore hats in the 40's and 50's. (I think there was legislation.)

Everyone called my dad "Mitch."

A Johnstown High graduate, he worked summers and holidays in the steel mill, and saved every cent for tuition. Mitch wanted to practice medicine.

This ambitious kid impressed the veteran steelworkers. Two, in particular, Mikey and Ninko, showed him the ropes and watched over him.

After completing pre-med at Pitt, he earned his doctorate at

Hahnemann Medical School in Philadelphia. Mitch met Dorothy, a Philly filly, and married her in 1946.

Now, 1958, Dad and his cronies gather in Morrellville. Mikey, Ninko, Milan, and Barney (another pal whose hats always had flashy, oversized bands), stand on the sidewalk, gawking, awestruck, at the most glamourous, magnetic, attention-grabbing gal they ever met.

Her name was Julie, a 1930 Model A Ford, purchased brand new by Ninko a week after she arrived at the dealership.

The fellas saw Julie plenty over the years, but she never failed to mesmerize them.

Garage kept, her shiny bronze body was immaculate. Her plush beige interior featured pockets on each door. A canvas patch protected her roof from luggage fastening. She had no trunk. She had a rumble seat. Shiny black fenders melted into running boards.

Mom disapproved of this wild bunch who played raucous weekly poker games in our basement rec room. I blame myself for getting them "evicted."

I'd hide in the stairwell to spy on this phenomenon. Men laughing, drinking, saying words like "deal, raise, full house, flush," fascinated 8 year old me.

Grown-ups were having *fun*. Grown-ups NEVER had fun!

Mitch promised his mill buds free medical care when he finished his education, and he was true to his word.

Every Sunday afternoon, he carried his black medical bag on house calls. He stocked meds, and refilled his supplies at Morrellville's Corner Drug Store. Sometimes he'd cross Fairfield Avenue and shop at Joe Beerman's Menswear, emerging with yet another ill-fitting pair of trousers.

But if he spotted Julie, he'd for sure stop at Milan's.

We lost Ninko in 1963.

He willed Julie to Mitch.

For two years, she sat at the end of our driveway. Dad loved to take friends and me for rides. We'd climb into the rumble seat and let the summer wind ruin our carefully-sprayed hairdos.

I worshipped that car, just like the old gang. I washed her, waxed her, vacuumed her interior, and dreamed of turning sixteen, when Julie and I would drive into the sunset.

Mom, however, put her foot down. A 1930 vehicle didn't have the reliability or safety features of a 60's car. She insisted Julie had to go.

No, I never asked my dad where she went. I know he missed her as much as I did. I'm certain he found her a good home.

But, please "honk" once today in her memory.

STAR-DUSTED BY CELEBRITIES

My starstruck mom doted on anything "Hollywood." We "drive-in-ed" whenever the feature changed. We bused downtown to indoor theaters. We rarely missed a show at our local arena.

Seasoned country comedienne Minnie Pearl brought her homespun humor to our War Memorial arena. Mom and I scored her autograph by waiting at the stage door. Minnie hugged me. I was 6.

Mom's sister, Aunt Ethel, lived on the fifth floor of an eight-story apartment building in Philadelphia. A real apartment, it featured a doorman, elevator, and locked mailboxes in the lobby.

Mom and I spent a week there when I was 9. One afternoon, Ethel handed me her key and sent me to fetch her mail.

How grown-up was THAT? Ride the elevator alone, greet the doorman, and unlock the box!

The elevator stopped at three and a familiar-looking man stepped in. I recognized him but couldn't place him.

"Hello, young lady," he said cordially.

"Hello."

In the lobby, the doorman rushed over. "Good afternoon, Mr. Bishop," he boomed.

"Oh my gosh!" I exclaimed. "That was Joey Bishop."

I dashed up five flights of steps. "I just rode the elevator with Joey Bishop!" I announced breathlessly.

My mother swooned.

Sophisticated Ethel said, "He's dating a lady on three. Where's the mail, Michele?"

I'd forgotten it.

In the 60's and 70's, Gary Puckett (of the "Union Gap") dominated my rock and roll fantasies. My favorite GP tune is "Over You," ("I guess there's just no getting...over yoouuu...!").

Hey, I never said I could sing.

Spring of '87 brought news that GP would appear at a local night club. I quickly made reservation.

Hubby and I arrived early. While we waited, I spotted GP striding across the dance floor to the bar.

"Look!" I pounded on Hubby's arm. "It's HIM! Gary Puckett!"

I crossed the room as gracefully as possible. "Gary Puckett?" I asked tentatively.

He smiled, sliding his drink along the bar. "Hello."

So much for restraint. "I have every one of your records," I gushed. "Your voice is awesome. Could I have your autograph?"

31

"Sure." He took a pen from his pocket and reached for a cardboard coaster. "What's your name?"

"Michele," I answered, "with one L."

He extended his hand for a "shake" and placed the coaster in my palm. I was TOUCHING Gary Puckett! I nearly burst an artery.

"Would you sing 'Over You' tonight?"

"I certainly will," he grinned. "Nice to meet you."

I floated back to our table. GP opened his show with "Over You."

"For my friend, Michele," he told the crowd. "With one L."

I saved my most poignant star-dusted memory for last.

In autumn '67, Peter, Paul, and Mary performed a concert in Pittsburgh, about 70 miles away from Johnstown. My friends and I explored downtown that afternoon.

In Kaufmann's, a small crowd had gathered by an area roped off in velvet.

"What's going on?" we asked.

"Mary's shopping," a woman whispered.

Sure enough Mary Travers, surrounded by a gaggle of clerks, stood browsing through formal wear.

Peter Yarrow and Paul Stookey sat nearby, fidgeting uncomfortably like Dagwood when Blondie drags him to Tudbury's. We watched, mesmerized.

Suddenly, Mary turned around. Our eyes locked. She smiled.

My mind reeled. Mary's smiling at me! What should I do? I had a split second.

I am a child of the 60's. I smiled back and flashed the Peace Sign.

Mary's smile grew brighter, and she returned the sign.

Peace to you, Mary, and peace to all.

A CLEAN GETAWAY

The concept of hibernation appeals to me tremendously. Curl up the day after New Year's, sleep until St. Patrick's Day maybe. Yeah, I could totally do that. When winds howl and snow flies, I prefer to hunker in.

Alas, bears and groundhogs have all the fun. We humans sometimes must battle the elements and, more often than not, we battle them to go…SHOPPING.

One long-ago winter, bronchitis sidelined me for about two weeks. Outdoors, snow drifted and temperatures plunged, so I didn't feel as if I missed much. However, indoors supplies of Tide, Kleenex, Listerine, Crest, and Irish Spring bar soap grew dangerously low.

Before the many dollar stores sprouted, I shopped for these items at gone-but-not-forgotten PharMor. Their discount prices lured me uphill despite the bluster of winter winds.

Then there was my mom's February birthday. Sears 'catalog made the gift selection easy. I spotted a sweater that I knew she'd love and phoned in my order.

Sears called on a day when the mercury crept toward 35. The sweater had arrived.

Skies, although gray, were not spewing snowflakes or sleet. It seemed as good a day as any to venture out. Still coughing and wheezing, I drove uptown.

PharMor's parking lot had melted to slush. Armed with my list, I entered the store, emerging about 20 minutes later with my sack full of necessities. I placed the bag on the floor on the passenger side.

Back then, Sears occupied a corner of our Mall. A small lot just outside the catalog department was designated for catalog shoppers. I cruised snow-covered aisles searching for an empty spot until I spied reverse lights. Someone was leaving.

I pulled near and waited patiently. The driver, a very elderly man, took five "back-ups" to vacate that slot. The second he cleared it, and just as I shifted back into "drive," two twenty-something guys driving a battered blue Chevy Nova whipped into the spot ahead of me.

I drove several rows back and finally found another opening. As I trudged over crunchy snow heading toward the store, steam poured out my ears. The young men watched me approach.

One spoke up. "Whatsamatter, lady? Did we steal your parking spot?"

Then the other chimed in. "We're sooo sorry. That wasn't nice at all."

Not satisfied with merely pilfering my spot, they felt compelled to taunt me.

They disappeared into the store. My catalog purchase took just minutes, and I returned to my car in no time.

As I placed Mom's sweater on the seat beside me, the PharMor bag caught my eye. There, on top of the household supplies, sat the four-pack of Irish Spring. Temptation overcame me. I unwrapped a bar.

I drove three rows up and stopped in front of the Nova. Clutching the Irish Spring, I walked over to their windshield.

"You weren't REALLY sorry," I scrawled across the glass in enormous waxy green letters. "But NOW you ARE!!"

Then I got back in my car and sped off. I made, you might say, a clean getaway.

EXPIRATION DATES SIGNAL THYME'S UP

Refrigerators look harmless, innocent, ordinary. But they have a dark side.

They often harbor questionable condiments, suspicious fruit, and potentially dangerous leftovers.

When you think about it, it's amazing that many of us are still alive.

'50's moms reached into the Philco to fetch the Oleo dish. It sat out on the table until after dinner. No one questioned the age of the Miracle Whip. Some folks refrigerated ketchup. Some didn't.

My Aunt Ethel grew up during the Depression. She rarely discarded anything. When she moved here from Philadelphia in '79, she brought 14 cartons of canned goods (some probably purchased during the Eisenhower administration).

Expiration dates, invented in the mid-80's, alert us to imminent spoilage. Before that, we just smelled stuff.

I'm convinced that fridges, in cahoots with grocery chains, allow "Label Gremlins" to sneak in at night and mess with dates. Targeting salad dressings, mayonnaise, butter and other perishables, they guilt us into higher food bills as we replace "out-dates."

Mom and I called Ethel's refrigerator "Jaws." When she traveled, we'd pounce on "Jaws," removing anything iffy or festering.

Once we held a "Name The Mystery Meat" contest. Friends and neighbors dropped quarters in a jar for a chance to identify 4 slices of decomposed lunchmeat sealed in a zip-lock bag.

Our friend Donna won the $2.75 pot by correctly guessing "Lebanon bologna."

The "Ethel Experience" taught me to be cautious around refrigerators.

In the mid-'70's, I owned a little house. I rented the spare bedroom to Jenny, a 26 year old college student who felt "too old" for dorm life. Part of our rental agreement included fridge space.

Unlike me, Jenny could cook.

She also liked "natural" beauty products and whipped up wrinkle treatments, exfoliants, and facial masks out of ingredients like yogurt, oregano, avocados, basil, mangos and persimmon. She always offered to share, but eating spicy dishes and smearing pulverized kiwi on my cheeks didn't work for me.

I possess no culinary talent. I had even LESS back then. Spaghetti and jar sauce, endless varieties of Tyson frozen bagged chicken, canned veggies, salads and Jello kept me alive.

That summer I dated Bud, who enthusiastically accepted my dinner invitations and enjoyed the meal as if it had been prepared for him by Julia Child.

One evening, Bud arrived early for our movie date. (Jenny went home to Altoona for the weekend.)

"Can I raid your fridge?" he yelled up the steps.

"Make yourself at home!" I laughed.

Five minutes later, I entered the kitchen. Bud, seated at the table, had a beer and the Tupperware container filled with Jenny's latest organic facial mask.

He was spreading the mixture on Ritz crackers. "Thish dip's great," he gulped through a mouthful. "You gotta show me how to make it!"

I never told him. But, of course, I had to tell Jenny.

She moved out shortly after. I'd "compromised her private space."

Boo Hoo! I think she just ran out of thyme.

ROADTRIP MEMORIES BUBBLE OVER

My friend Carolyn invited me to a church festival. We had a great time.

"They have handicap parking," she assured me. "Turn at the light by the church, and drive around back. I'll watch for you. What kind of car do you drive?"

"A PT Cruiser, a 'woody.' I named Bailey for his color, just like Bailey's Irish Cream."

"You *name* your cars?" she asked.

"Oh, yes," I replied.

The first car I ever met who had a name was Julie, a Model A Ford. Ninko, Dad's buddy, drove her, brand new, out of the showroom in 1930. Julie introduced me to radiator caps, running boards, and rumble seats, slices of automotive history.

Neighbors named my rusty, tired Dodge "The Wonder Car." They wondered what kept it running. Big, green, and ugly, "The Hulk," a '73 Chevy station wagon, helped me move twice.

In 1987, Hubby bought a 1980 Cadillac Sedan DeVille. "Me? Drive this? Caddy folks lunch at the club and listen to opera. I prefer drive-up windows and The Ronettes."

But it grew on me. A rich shade of burgundy, it featured a plush, velour interior and ginormous trunk. With a 142 inch wheelbase, it had the turning radius of the Titanic.

A car wash boasting a self-serve area with gizmos galore had just opened. Pre-wash, under spray, foam brush...whoa! *Foambrush* ? It spewed tons of luxurious pink foam. Frothy bubbles shrouded my huge car. How cool was this?

"Beeep! Cycle has ended. Insert additional coins for rinse," a mechanical voice droned. I didn't have enough change. No other human was at this 'auto-automat.' I could *not* rinse.

Mom lived nearby. I decided to flee. Picture a massive vehicle covered in pink suds creeping down the highway. Breezes caught chunks of lather and dropped them on hoods and windshields of amazed motorists.

As I rinsed the car with Mom's garden hose, I realized only one name would suit the Caddy and commemorate our adventure. I christened her "Bubbles."

In the late '80's, I acted as caregiver for Mom; her sister Ethel; my dad's sister "Aunt Sis;"and Sis's best friend and nursing home roomie, Helen. Bubbles' ample interior provided a comfy ride and her trunk held walkers, canes, and wheelchairs.

One scorching summer day, Ethel had a doctor's appointment. Mom called me. "On your way back, stop at the home and get Sis and Helen. I'll have dinner ready on the patio."

Approaching a busy intersection, I discovered I had no brakes. I steered into an empty church parking lot and stopped Bubbles with the emergency brake.

"Why are we stopping?" demanded Sis.

"Are we there yet?" wondered Helen.

"Bubbles broke down," I answered. "I'm going to find a phone. Open the doors but *don't get out!*"

I spotted a police car at the light and waved frantically. The girls all yammered at once as the cruiser pulled next to us.

"My brakes gave out. Could you give me a ride to Westwood? I can get my mom's car."

"Only Westwood? I'll take all of you," he offered. "This heat's too much for them."

"Thank you so much," I gushed.

Sis, Ethel and Helen slid into the rear seat behind the cage while the officer and I transferred their gear to his trunk.

I sat up front and looked wistfully at the 'kennel' behind me. "Do you think I could get one of those for my car?"

"What if Dorothy sees us arrive in a police car?" worried Ethel. "She'll have a stroke!"

Sis, thoroughly enjoying herself, tapped me on the shoulder. "Hey, girlie, what're you in for?"

"Drunk and disorderly. How about you?"

"Aw, we got busted turning tricks at the nursing home."

I thought the policeman's head would explode.

"Turn here," I pointed.
"Women's Detention Center!" I announced. "Everybody out!"
"Thank you again," I told him. "And I'll call a tow truck for Bubbles."
"'Bubbles'? You named your car 'Bubbles?'" He looked dumbfounded.
"Long story." I winked at him. "Another time."

CHAPTER 4: HEAVEN SMILED

THEY SHOOT BRIDESMAIDS, DON'T THEY?

In February, wedding showcases pop up everywhere. Let's talk bridesmaids' dresses.

Legend tells us that when Cinderella became engaged to Prince Charming, she immediately started planning her wedding. Designating her stepsisters as bridesmaids, she scoured the kingdom in search of the ugliest gowns imaginable.

Many women believe this tradition lives on.

My friend Debbie had the worst gown I ever saw.

Maid of Honor at her cousin's winter wedding, she wore dark green velvet with a garish lime green satin belt around the empire waist! A ruffle in the same awful shade framed the neckline and cuffs (think Clarabelle, the clown from Howdy Doody).

In Johnstown during the 60's and 70's, if you wanted custom bridal apparel, you shopped at Jeanine's. On Main Street, occupying the second floor above the Singer Sewing Center, the little boutique outfitted brides and their attendants for twenty years.

For my formal wedding, I made my own gown. It cost $37.50.

I sent my friends, Sharon and Cincinnati Cathy, to Jeanine's to select their gowns. They chose long satin with a chiffon overlay and puffy sleeves. Cathy liked pink and Sharon, yellow.

Years later, Sharon complained that she looked like Sesame Street's Big Bird that day.

"You picked 'em," I reminded her. "Any pain you suffered was self-inflicted!"

In 1972, Sharon was married in a mini-dress. I wore a green cocktail dress from my closet.

My next bridesmaid gig came twenty-five years later.

We had lovely royal blue gowns, but shoes remained up to us.

At 5 foot 10, I never even consider high heels. I prowled shoe stores seeking dye-able satin flats. I shop in the "Sasquatch Dept" for my size 10 wides!

The wedding planner taught us the formal promenade: right foot step...pause; left foot step...pause. I practiced at home, but still kept favoring my right foot, lurching like Quasimoto.

Our gaggle of bridesmaids dressed in a Sunday School classroom. The church was next door. We had to walk outside.

Alas, while we primped, it poured. Water ponded heavily over the sidewalk. By the time we reached the vestibule, my flats had absorbed about 8 gallons and weighed probably five pounds each.

I started my promenade: right foot step, slosh...pause, squish; left foot step, slosh... .

Halfway there, one of my saturated shoes fell off. I maneuvered near the pews where a lady retrieved it, discreetly placing it on my foot, like re-shoeing Secretariat midway through the Preakness.

Then she looked at her hand in horror; her thumb and index finger were royal blue! No good deed goes unpunished.

A few years back, an idea struck me for reusing those dresses.

I threw a costume party, "The Ugly Stepsisters' Ball." Women wore old bridesmaids' gowns, and men wore anything in bad taste. My guests loved it, and everyone had, well...a BALL!

Cinderella would have approved.

PUTTING THE FUN IN FUNERAL

I will never forget my Grandma Tootsie's funeral.

Tootsie, my dad's stepmom, died when I was eight. My dad, my uncles, and Aunt Sis never liked her.

I don't know whether she was an "evil stepmother" or not. I only knew her house smelled like lilacs, and handmade lace doilies covered every surface.

The family held a meeting and decided kids eight and older would attend the funeral. I made the cut. I was about to see my first dead person.

The Orthodox funeral rite is a beautiful, solemn ceremony steeped in tradition, probably a fitting way to introduce eight-year-old me to life's passages.

Closest family members sit in the front pews. Friends and neighbors sit in the rear. Everyone receives a candle. The service ends with a procession. Folks file past the open casket and light their tapers from a large one at the altar.

I didn't light mine, but no one seemed to mind.

My dad, mom, and I sat in the third row.

Tootsie's sisters from Cleveland, seated in the first row, were last in the procession.

Suddenly, one of them snapped. "Mary! Mary! Take me with you!" she wailed, and dived into the casket with Tootsie.

I sat wide-eyed, aghast. "Wow! So THIS is a funeral!"

Then my father spoke, in a booming voice loud enough to be heard clearly over the commotion. "Shut the lid," he said.

My mom glared at him. Then she blew out her candle, tossed it on the pew, grabbed me by the hand, and stormed out of the church. For us, the funeral had ended.

Reincarnation fascinates me. If it exists, I'd like to come back as a mermaid. Think about it…swim in warm water all day, enjoy an endless supply of shellfish, never have a bad hair day, and never need to shave your legs.

At a recent viewing I attended, I sat reminiscing with a group of friends.

"Too bad you can't hear all the nice things people say about you after you're gone," observed one.

"I'd like people to recognize my professional accomplishments," said another.

"I want to be remembered as a loving mother and grandmother," someone else chimed in. "How about you, Michele?" she added. "What would you like people to say about you at your viewing?"

I thought about that for a minute. Then I smiled. "Most of all, I'd like someone in the room to say, 'Look! She's MOVING!'"

REMEMBERING SISTER BAMBI

For thirteen years I sold refreshment tickets at our three annual summer church festivals. Most folks purchased $5 or $10 worth at a clip, but others expressed concern about being "stuck" with unused tickets after the event.

"You're never 'stuck' with them," I'd assure my customers. "The tickets are good from festival to festival and year to year. We're church," I'd add. "We do ETERNITY!"

Apparently, I was wrong. Attendance has dwindled. The majestic buildings ring up high utility bills. Aging sanctuaries require extensive repairs and maintenance. The Diocese decided to merge five of the congregations into one building.

At 11:59 July 21, my St. .Rochus Church was "suppressed."

My grandfather, an immigrant from Croatia, helped build St. Rochus. My dad, all his brothers, and Aunt Sis attended the Rochus school.

You believe your church will always be there for you. Confessions, communions, confirmations, funerals, fish fries, festivals, fellowship – everything that sustains us.

Father Charlie led our flock with faith, wisdom, and humor. Church secretary Joann dazzled us with her awesome multi-tasking competence. Music Dude directed our choir for 8 years. I called Father and him "The Righteous Brothers" because they brought us "blue-eyed soul."

I first volunteered as a cashier at the fish fries. We'd been serving haddock for thirty years, but weekly someone would inquire, "What type of fish is that?"

I begged Joann, " Just once, let me answer. 'Today, we have a squid special, and for children, peanut butter and jellyfish sandwiches.'"

Our famous homemade dessert buffet highlighted the fish fries for many people.

One lady fretted over the rich, tempting goodies. "Those desserts are my downfall," she sighed after ordering healthy broiled fish.

"Don't worry," I smiled. " Father always blesses the desserts. It neutralizes the calories."

Next, I started to help out at the rectory office.

"When you work at a church," Joann told me, "strangers think you're a nun. I love jewelry and always do my nails, but still some new delivery person will say 'Thank you, Sister.'"

One afternoon, a man arrived looking for Father. Joann took the fellow's name and number. Then he began to ramble on, describing his problems in detail.

Poor Joann listened politely, a captive audience. I continued with my tasks. Every time I moved, the guy stared at me. He gave me the willies.

Finally, he left. "Michele," laughed Joann, "that fella was checkin' you out! There's your next husband!"

"Joann, if that guy ever comes back and asks anything about me, you tell him I'M A NUN!"

When Father returned, we told him the tale. "If you're a nun, you need a name," he reasoned. "How about Sister Bambi?"

Joann howled. "What order do you belong to, Sister?"

"The Sisters of Peroxide," I answered.

Back then, we had two nuns in residence. One day I met them in the courtyard. "Hey, Sister Bernadette, Sister Wilma!" I called.

"Hey, Sister Bambi!" Wilma replied with a wink.

St. Rochus, I will miss you.

RIGGIES, PIGGIES, AND DIGGIES

February brings Bridal Fairs. Bargain-hunting grooms prowl Valentine ring sales, while brides-to-be lose all touch with reality. Swept beneath an avalanche of colors, menus, cakes, reception halls, limos and, of course, gowns, normal maidens morph into Bridezillas…obsessed, stressed, possessed, and probably a few more S words.

Many brides haven't noticed that our economy has tanked. Don't believe me? Tune in to The Learning Channel on Thursday or Friday evenings and watch a program called "Say YES to the Dress."

"The Learning Channel" sounds dignified, informative, and edifying. It shocks viewers to discover their programming includes "Toddlers in Tiaras," Hoarding: Buried Alive," "Amish Mafia" and "Long Island Medium." That certainly expands MY horizons.

I can't pinpoint when women went wedding-wacko, but it's been going on for at least 15 years. I blame Princess Diana, although she probably needed all that pageantry to distract her from marrying a mama's boy whose ears look like back doors left open on a taxicab.

I made my formal wedding gown. It cost $37.50. A popular local reception venue charged $500 for the reception (100 people). My bridesmaids, Sharon and Cincinnati Cathy, purchased their dresses at Jeanine's, a little wedding boutique on the second floor above the Singer Sewing Center on Main Street.

The "Say Yes" show stars an elfin creature named Randy who operates a posh Beverly Hills Bridal Boutique. The women seem normal until they reveal their dress budgets…$2,500; $6,000, $12,000, and up. They usually bring a gaggle of friends and relatives, which almost guarantees dissention.

The most extravagant gal bought an $18,500 gown. Her final tab rose to $22,900 when she added a $4000 veil and $1400 train!

My first house cost $23,500!

Another bride bought TWO gowns, one for the ceremony and a racier one for the reception!

We dial back the extravagance here in PA.

Johnstown receptions begin with veggie trays, meat and cheese cube platters and dozens of homemade cookies baked by aunts and Grandmas.

Wedding feasts feature yummy ethnic specialties, usually riggies, piggies, and diggies (rigatoni, pigs in the blanket, and chicken wings to dip). A $199 David's Bridal frock transforms any gal into an enchantress.

I recall 2 unforgettable weddings, one where the groom vanished! The money dance ended, yet the weary band started the 38th chorus of "Da da dadada DA da…"

The exhausted bride collapsed in a folding chair, weeping.

Suddenly, 4 huge guys burst in, carrying the motionless groom. They opened a side door and slid his carcass into the back of an SUV. He clearly had been "over-served."

A DJ spoiled another infamous reception. Bikers gathered at a rural firehall to celebrate some Harley nuptials. The DJ brought his 12 year old daughter to "help."

He arrived hammered. The guests were tolerant until he began staggering, bumping into stuff, and pawing women.

His daughter bravely kept the music playing. Finally, he crashed into a table, breaking some dishes. The girl ran to his aide, and he angrily blamed her, smacking her and sending her flying.

Child abuse lights bikers up. Behavior like that rankles everybody, but bikers spark off like M-80's.

The guests that weren't arrested continued the party at a tavern down the road.

And, yeah, we took some cookies, cake, a bag of chips and a centerpiece.

I mean, after all, we did give them a "Mr.Coffee."

CHAPTER 5: IN SICKNESS AND IN HEALTH

THE HOSPITAL EVOLVED

As I kid, if I needed medical help, I just yelled "Dad!" He treated coughs, colds, boo-boos (stitches…yuk), administered vaccinations , and more.

Occasionally, if he received an emergency call, he took me along. I visited with nurses at their station while he tended a patient. I think he was trying to steer me toward a nursing career.

He always had a "doctor job": administration or supervision at other medical facilities. He saw patients at our local Catholic hospital, Mercy.

A doctor pal of his removed my tonsils in 1957. I was eight. My first ever hospital stay fascinated me. I absorbed every sight, sound, smell, and touch like a sponge. Tastes, not so much. It was, after all, a tonsillectomy.

Nurses wore crisp white uniforms and caps. Everything smelled like alcohol or disinfectant. My bed had a crank. ETHER sedated me for the operation.

Twenty years later, I returned to Mercy for another surgery. Doctors found a lump near my throat. My surgeon, another of dad's cronies, took excellent care of me.

But medical technology was evolving. Beds were electric. Smells weren't as intense. More good news: ether was gone.

My lump was benign, but it signaled the onset of an illness that's kept me on a scary roller-coaster ride through the healthcare system for almost 50 years.

My dad died in 1984. I stumbled onto a compassionate, amazing primary care physician who's kept me kicking since then.

In 2010, my white blood cells dropped to a dangerously low level.

"It's time to send you to the 'Big House,'" explained my doctor.

I saw it coming. I was weak, tired, had no appetite, and was dizzier than usual. Plus, there were freaky, weird dreams.

One night I dreamed my laundry jumped out of the hamper, singing and dancing. My socks had little stick arms and legs and did kicks like the Rockettes.

Over time, Mercy and Memorial, located next door to each other, merged. Patients balked at first, but soon realized that duplication of services in such close proximity increased costs. Departmentalizing allowed purchases of high-end equipment and more detailed diagnoses and treatment.

Talk about coming full circle, I was admitted to the 4th floor of Good Samaritan which is the former Mercy. If a hospital can be "home," I was there.

Compassionate caregivers wearing colorful scrubs took excellent care of me. These ladies and gentlemen, who clearly worked as a team for a long time, complimented each other's strengths.

I tried their patience. Any more "whine" and we'd have needed a Wisconsin cheese catalog.

Progress marches on. Advancements dazzled me.

The electric beds now gently vibrate to prevent bed sores. Housekeeping kept my room spotless without any scary odors.

No more food trays with broth, Jello, and a slice of Wonder bread in a baggie; a menu showcasing gourmet-quality food awakened my dormant appetite.

Hospital personnel performed numerous tests and finally tracked my blood ailment back to a viral infection, yet another "bump" on the coaster.

Six days later, I "graduated."

God bless the precious folks who gave me their best, RN's and staff. Their help was indeed a blessing.

"Mercifully," my entire hospital experience was positive. I know how lucky I am. The changes I have witnessed in fifty years are incredible.

I have only one question. They can valet park you, scan you, MRI you, gourmet feed you…can't they do something about those gowns?

A LA CARTE

When we reach our fifties we learn, to our chagrin, that warranties on certain body parts have pretty much run out. My friends and I encounter this more and more.

Legs and feet seem particularly vulnerable. Myself, I must use a cane and, for long distances, a wheelchair. Other folks require more invasive solutions: my friend, Cincinnati Cathy, sports a new titanium hip that activates the metal detector at her local Walgreen's.

Fortunately for us rapidly deteriorating geezers and geezerettes, some stores now provide electric carts to transport our baby boomer fannies through their aisles.

Our old Walmart was roughly the size of Connecticut. When they announced their plan to become a Supercenter with the acreage of, say, Oklahoma, I realized my days of feebly tottering from department to department had ended.

For those of you who have never driven a cart, here's the scoop: they don't have brakes, only GO and DON'T GO.

I "trained" out of town, choosing Altoona where no one would know me. That turned out to be a swell idea.

Just a month before Christmas, the store overflowed with merchandise. I crashed into at least a half-dozen displays before I learned to back off GO and coast the remaining 6 or so inches to stop.

As I filled my basket, my confidence soared. Shopping at 20 mph! Cool!

Then my purse strap became tangled around GO. Full throttle and unable to steer, I careened toward the snack bar. Terrified diners abandoned burgers and fries to flee from my path. My rampage ended when I smacked into the wall by the service desk.

The "greeter" rushed to my aid. I detected his spirit momentarily leaving his body.

I can proudly report that my technique has vastly improved. I haven't whacked a display or terrorized a shopper in 3 years.

During my most recent expedition, I ran across another cart rider. We compared our handicaps: she suffered from rheumatoid arthritis. I challenged her to a drag race in the deserted frozen food aisle.

However, I must pay closer to what I wear. I'm a "dresses only" kind of gal, and prefer ones with long, full skirts.

Last May, I shopped in blue cotton with a ruffle. When I reached the check-out, I discovered my dangling ruffle had swept the entire store. Dirt, grass, and dust bunnies lodged in my hem.

It became my "Swiffer dress."

I love Walmart Online Mail Order. A bigger selection, free shipping and privacy saves me money and sanity. I still shop in person once or twice a year, generally spring and fall.

So, watch out ! I'll be the one lurching at you in a "Rascal," shopping at the speed of sound.

You've been warned.

HIP HIP HOORAY

"How," asked my cousin Tanya on the phone, "could you break your *left* foot and your *right* hip?"

"I fainted," I told her, shifting painfully in my hospital bed. "It's hard to do damage control if you're unconscious."

A case of flu had exhausted me the week before. I battled sniffles, chills, fevers, barfs, and dizzies. By Thursday, I expected to cough up a lung.

Friday March 6, I fainted. It wasn't glamorous or romantic, like Miss Scarlett getting "the vapors." I woke up wrapped around my walker like a pretzel.

I was expecting galpal Leanne at 9:30, so I rolled over and tried to get up. Talk about pain! Leanne called my friend Joe.

He arrived with my wheelchair and his dog, Licorice. Even a big "poochie moochie" didn't help. "Team Bender" situated my sorry arse in the car. Licorice snuggled close to me. She smelled trouble.

The hospital staff had clearly seen many broken hips. This was NOT their first rodeo. After a quick once-over, an ER doctor ordered tests. My injuries were so extensive that *one* test wouldn't do it. I needed MRI's and ultra-sound.

By 8pm, I settled into my 9th floor room.

Dr. D peeked in the door. "You broke your hip," he announced.

"#%&$@!!" I answered.

"Operation at noon tomorrow," he added and disappeared down the hall.

9th floor personnel cared for me that night. The next morning, phlebotomists did endless bloodwork. A skillful IV lady inserted my lock.

I rode to the OR...and BACK...in my *own* bed! They put me to sleep to eliminate the pain of 4 transfers.

Dr. D stopped in Saturday evening. "We had to replace your whole hip," he explained.

I was speechless, and you know how often THAT happens!

I rested Sunday, but staffers all pitched in to get me moving on Monday.

The respiratory therapist taught me how to blow in to tubes and make moth balls rattle. A cardio physician's assistant made sure "the beat went on!"

Despite all the activity, housekeepers kept my room sparkling, and dieticians delivered tasty meals.

A trauma lady, supervised my progress. Therapy ladies visited twice daily and had me standing, sitting and walking by Tuesday! Magic!

I have always been pigeon-toed, but the hip break made it worse. Hospitals, however, fix *everything!*

Saturday night after the operation, nurses brought in a big Styrofoam gismo. It looked like a Penn Dot traffic cone (except for the styrofoam part) and...it was PINK!

The nurses pushed it between my legs and, using Velcro bands, strapped my floppy right ankle and disobedient knee to this inflexible contraption, binding both securely in place.

Kinky, eh? A little orthopedic S & M!

My hospital trip ended when they sent me to rehab in the former Lee Hospital building. I was delighted...ready for the next level.

After 6 days on the 9th floor, an evaluator from the Trauma Dept., stopped to talk. "Michele, only sick people belong in hospitals. You're not sick; you're *injured.* You're ready for the next care level."

"I understand," I replied, and I did. This wouldn't be my first rehab rodeo. I was headed to our former center town hospital that now housed a rehab center. My dad's office sat right where the hospital circle is today. I have a soft spot for Lincoln St.

The progress I made in mobility in only 6 days amazed me. My mom broke her hip in 1987, and suffered through agonizing months of recovery.

I discovered a gym full of equipment, everything from cots and wedges to spinbikes and weights.

Best of all, a skilled, congenial, warmhearted staff stood by to capably and patiently assist us as we struggled. The same bunch celebrated our triumphs and bolstered our optimism.

Physical therapists supervised my exercises in the gym. Occupational therapists explained my limitations dealing with every day activities (dressing, showers, etc). I learned specific precautions to take so as not to damage my hip in its early stages of healing.

My new hip is ceramic. The image of art class, where we fashioned ash trays and flower pots out of clay, didn't reinforce my sense of security. Little, breakable figures – Hummels! Do they still MAKE those?

I consider my new hip *porcelain*. Picture those steamy commercials for Moen and Kohler where couples romp around the porcelain facilities in their bathrooms. That's resilient!

Of course, Medicare paid for it. (Your tax dollars at work! I thank you!)

I deeply appreciated the skillful, healing hands of my compassionate caregivers.

In the 50's, my dad was a staff chief at Mercy Hospital. He later expanded his practice and saw patients at Lee.

Then Mercy and Lee "morphed" into Conemaugh Medical Center, creating a rehab center at Lee.

Somewhere on his cloud, my dad is smiling.

DIVING FOR TREASURE IN THE GENE POOL

Father Jim, a hospital chaplain, stood in my doorway. "Are you here AGAIN?"

"I come for the food," I grinned. "I can't resist the stewed tomatoes!"

Yes, here I sit writing about yet another hospitalization.

When my friend Sharon called, I quizzed her. "Do you think another column about my ailments will bore my readers?"

"You're kidding, right?" she laughed. "Your readers are OUR age! They deal with illness, too. They'll LOVE it!"

Most folks have a fairly healthy gene pool. I have a septic tank.

My ancestors suffered from a cornucopia of maladies. Over the past two years, I've flirted with pretty much all of them. I've become a familiar face at our hospital.

Highmark gives me Cash Back Bonus points and I've accumulated "frequent ambulance rider" miles. A "Reconstructed Vehicle" title has replaced my birth certificate.

Have you ever had a kidney stone? You'd remember if you had! A potpourri of dandy complications accompanies them as well: continuous pressure, burning, and, well…other issues. (Don't make me say it!)

It seems I've blazed the genetic trail to the kidney stone quarry. Apparently, I'm the first "stoner" in our family.

Most kidney stones disintegrate simply during a procedure called "lipotripsy." My indestructible cinders consisted of kryptonite reinforced with Rustoleum.

These impenetrable boulders frustrated my urologist, Dr. F, but he and his amazing staff rose to the challenge and answered my zillion questions.

Dr. F even drew a diagram of my "innards." I posted it on the bulletin board in my hospital room (I didn't have a fridge or magnets handy!).

His physician's assistant said he'd observed more troublesome stones among baby boomers. Could this be backlash from our misspent youth?

My journeys always began in Outpatient Surgery where nurses prepped me and kept me calm. Anesthesiologists and an O.R. nurse guided me through my adventures.

Phlebotomists and IV nurses gently "needled" me.

With luck, no more "pebbles" will rattle my guts.

Let's hope that any stones in my future will be the type measured in carats!

THE SCENIC ROUTE TO RECOVERY

I thought it was this busy summer that wore me out. Father's Day afternoon I flopped in my recliner and forced myself to do some bookkeeping. I licked an envelope and gasped! No spit…blood…as if Hannibal Lechter just served me lunch.

I didn't cough or barf; my mouth just looked like the Bride of Dracula.

"Vampires are trendy this season," I told the paramedic with the ambulance crew.

The ER overflowed. Apparently many folks excessively and over-zealously celebrated the holiday. God bless the precious workers who signed us in, triaged us, and patched up those they could.

ER hustled me up to the 6th floor where I met the warm, caring crew who guided me through the next 9 days. Lab ladies battled my uncooperative veins to draw blood and insert IV's.

Transporters gently delivered me to areas where technicians

administered "alphabet tests…EKGs, MRI's and X-Rays."

I returned home Mon June 23. Doctors concluded that my too-thin blood caused my pressure to tank, creating other complications. They were close.

I still lacked energy, and sensed that something more was amiss.

Most families have gene pools to blame for illness hand-me-downs. I emerged from a septic tank. My ancestors suffered from a varied menu of maladies, but it seems I blazed the genetic trail to the kidney stone quarry. I am my family's first "STONER."

Two years earlier, Dr.F and his team fought my indestructible pebbles, composed of kryptonite coated in Rustoleum. We thought we won. But now, a renegade chip had broken off, blocked a vital duct, and given me blood-poisoning.

I experienced ICU for the first time. The staff members dazzled me with expertise and efficiency. Next, I moved to 8, where I remained until July 10.

The IV ladies faced my veins again. "Is there a special spot you'd like to try?" asked one, IV lock in her hand.

"Yes!" I suggested. "Let's use YOUR arm!"

After a physical therapy hike, I glanced out and spotted 4 construction workers on a roof across the street. A born rascal, I try to spread mischief wherever I go.

"Look!" I pointed. Three gals clustered with me at the window.

"What's up?" asked another, joining us.

"That guy with the hat is HOT!" I exclaimed.

"You're baaad!" they laughed.

"I believe," I smiled, "that the road to recovery should be 'scenic.'"

BLOOM WHERE YOU'RE PLANTED

"Ms. Bender? Are you awake?"

The guy sounded cute. I opened one eye.

"I'm Dr.S. I'll be your brain surgeon."

THAT opened BOTH EYES.

"Don't panic. You're experiencing slight bleeding in your brain, but you don't need surgery." He smiled reassuringly. "You have a small lesion but we can treat it with medicine."

So, it's really true! Tests over the course of 6 months have concluded that I DO have a brain. Apparently, it just leaks occasionally.

Strong medicines clouded my memories of 3 days in ICU, but the angels who cared for me will remain in my heart.

This was my second Christmas in a hospital. Elegant, tasteful decorations decked the halls..

My family doctor appeared the fourth day. He'd ordered additional tests with great results. No new blood clots popped in my legs, and residual damage from prior incidents was mending.

EXERCISE WORKS! WHO KNEW?

Hospital staffs go out of their ways to promote holiday cheer. The nurses and staff wore colorful, seasonal scrubs to make us smile. Some sported pins and barrettes with blinking lights to brighten the atmosphere.

My 4 physical therapy wizards took motion range and flexibility very seriously. They introduced us to outdoor therapy. They led us to the roof and taught us to rotate Santa's reindeer so they'd wear evenly.

The food is still delicious! I coerced the stewed tomato recipe out of a helper, but I still need the one for "spinach chicken Alfredo flatbread."
. That dish rocked!

Our comfort and dignity remained foremost concerns of every employee.

One morning as I was bird-bathing, a flustered aide dashed in and grabbed for my curtain!

"Hon, what's wrong?"

"Your curtain's open! Someone could see in."

"Don't worry," I reassured her. "Anyone who wants a glimpse of my fanny badly enough to scale the side of this 10 story building has definitely EARNED HIS PEEK!"

When I was 12, we moved. I was inconsolable. I loved my old house, my room, my neighborhood.

My Aunt Gertie told me, "Girl, bloom where you're planted.

May stardust and good health shine on your garden.

CHAPTER 6: CRITTERS

MY FAVORITE RED-HEAD

Peanuts' Charlie Brown yearned for "the little red-haired girl." Desi loved Lucy.

My favorite red-head had four legs and a tail. This Irish Setter was one year old when I brought her home long ago.

The shelter staff said her name was Kelly, but I changed that. The first red-haired person I ever met was a girl named Bridget in kindergarten. Kelly became Bridget.

Bridget was a human soul in a canine body. I called her my hairy little person. She watched what people did and did the same.

She slept in bed with her head on a pillow. On the sofa, she sat with her tail, fanny, and hind legs on the cushion, and front legs on the floor, people-style.

The only thing she loved more than long walks was car rides. She'd jump in right behind the wheel.

"Are you going to drive or shall I?" I'd ask.

If she'd had her own car, she would never have been home.

Apparently, Bridget had a colorful past. She wasn't talking, but actions speak louder. The minute she'd hear a snap top, she was THERE. Her nose told her what cans contained. Soda bored her, but suds made that tail dance.

I never gave her sips and I didn't allow guests to, but my little boozehound clearly knew what she was missing.

In addition to being quirky, she was amazingly smart.

Walking in the woods off the leash one afternoon, she spotted a chipmunk on a tree limb. She plucked him off the branch like he was an apple and turned to show me her trophy. His little arms and legs flailed.

"Bridget," I scolded, "spit him out this instant!"

"Pffft," she spat, and the frightened critter scampered back up the tree, probably saying a grateful chipmunk rosary.

Bridget had three boyfriends, two canine and one human. Casey, an Irish Wolfhound, and his "mom" often took leash walks with us. She admired Shiloh, a German Shepherd, from afar.

One night, I hooked her to her cable in the yard for a final "out." When I returned five minutes later, she was gone. I panicked.

I phoned my neighbor Dick. "Please help me find her!" I pleaded.

"I'll be right there," he promised.

I waited anxiously on my stoop and watched as his car passed beneath the street light. I saw two silhouettes, Dick behind the wheel and someone with long hair snuggled next to him.

"Darn! He has a date! I interrupted them!" I thought.

Dick opened his car door and flashed a huge grin. Then his "date" hopped out. It was Bridget!

"I found her in my yard," he explained.

"C'mon, let's go in and get a beer," I offered. I wagged my finger at Bridget. "No beer for you!"

SLINKY TAKES A RIDE

Snakes scare the daylights out of me. I know some people find them fascinating. I'm not one of them.

When I was twelve, we lived close to a dense forest. One afternoon I decided to bike to a friend's house. I raised our garage door, wheeled my Schwinn out front and went inside to tell mom I was leaving.

When I came out, a long black tubular thing lay next to my front wheel.

"Awww," I muttered, "a flat tire!"

Then the tire looked at me and extended its reptilian tongue.

"Snake!" I screamed, sprinting back through the garage and heaving the kitchen door open. "Snake!"

Mom came running and we did a "duet," both shrieking "Help! Snake!" until a neighbor rescued us by clobbering the intruder with a golf club.

The concept of snakes as pets completely baffles me.

Three years ago, an auto accident occurred involving an area woman and her pet snake. The newspaper reported that the woman crashed while driving down the road with the snake in her car.

A photo accompanied the story, showing police and emergency personnel held temporarily at bay by the snake, who apparently slithered from the wreckage and hovered nearby.

This news item made my imagination run wild.

Does a snake KNOW if he's in a car? Do you place him in a carrier like a cat, or simply call "Heeere, Slinky, wanna go byes?" How does he indicate interest? Does he wag his tail? Does he rattle? Does he perhaps gleefully extend his snaky little tongue?

Where do you take him? Do you drive him along on routine errands? "Okay, Slinky, now you behave here in the car while I run in Rite Aid."

What constitutes good snake behavior? Not slithering out the window and creating panic in the parking lot? Not constantly asking "Are we THERE yet?" How does he know IF you are there yet?

If he behaves, how do you reward him? Do you take him for ice cream?

Or maybe..."Good boy, Slinky. Let's buzz over to the pet delicacy shop and buy you a plump, tasty hamster!" Would he prefer it with hot fudge, or in a cone?

Do you pat him? Where do you pat him? Does he know he's being patted?

As you cruise along, does he hang his head out the window, forked tongue flapping in the breeze? Does he insist on his favorite music? "Okay, Slinky, I'll play the "Ozzie" CD one more time."

Does he get frightened when you go through the car wash?

What about road trips he'd rather NOT take? "Don't make me come in that closet after you, Slinky! Your vet appointment is two-thirty!"

What happens at the vet's office? Does he get immunized? How do they locate his fanny to administer the shot? How do they take his temperature? "Slinky, I *told* you, the thermometer goes UNDER your tongue!"

How about the dentist? "Great exam, Slinky! No cavities! You can spit now!"

I wonder if Slinky's owner showed him his picture on the front page of the paper. Maybe she reads the article over and over to him at bedtime, like a Dr. Seuss tale. I picture Slinky drifting off to sleep nightly with a smile on his lips.

Do snakes have lips? Do they smile? How can you tell they're smiling?

I need to stop now.

WHO'S HOGGIN' THE DECK?

I lived in a quaint neighborhood years ago. It boasted city ambiance. Sidewalks lined curbed streets and the transit bus rumbled by hourly. You'd think all these city amenities would intimidate wildlife. You'd be wrong.

Rabbits arrived first after we constructed a deck many summers past. They built four major tunnel entrances to their subterranean domain. If we attempted to seal one off, it reopened within hours. I believe a whole bunny metropolis lurked beneath my deck, with freeways, condos, and a mall or two.

Each spring, patient mama rabbits instructed their offspring in self-defense tactics. "That dog can run the deck in six seconds," warned Mama, clutching a stopwatch. "You don't leave this hole until you can run it in three!"

For two seasons, we hosted a chipmunk whom we named Floyd. Each day at 5:30, we served five peanuts to our guest, five being maximum chipmunk jaw capacity. If we were late, we heard about it. Floyd would pose on his hind legs, "hands" on his little chipmunk hips, and chatter angrily at the back door until we came across.

Once he caught another chipmunk filching his nuts. Floyd kicked chipmunk butt that day, using moves that would have dazzled Bruce Lee. Floyd was no slouch.

Suddenly, though, he vanished. I suspect something he disagreed with ate him..

The critter parade continued over the years. Squirrels, skunks, raccoons and a bat or two dropped by for visits of various lengths. But by far, the boldest of all was a groundhog who announced himself by stretching out next to a chaise lounge on the deck one summer morning.

He expanded the bunnies' entrances considerably. We presumed they fled.

Contrary to the images of loveable Gus, who sells us our lottery tickets, and cuddly Phil, who predicts our weather, non-celebrity groundhogs are irritable, territorial, and downright nasty.

A neighbor's teen stood in the next yard clapping, stomping and hollering, hoping to scare him off.

The groundhog was not impressed. He yawned and resumed his sunbath.

He disappeared that afternoon, and all of us in the 'hood hoped he had relocated. No such luck. The following morning he was reclining on my next door neighbor's back steps.

Folks with children expressed concern. One guy even went to fetch his shotgun. We warned him about the consequences of firing a weapon in the borough, and also reminded him that he'd be racked with guilt forever if he committed (Get ready...here it comes...) HOGICIDE ! We planned to call an exterminator.

The groundhog must have had a premonition of impending doom because he split that afternoon, never to return. Indeed, on his part, that was one lucky move.

SULLIVAN'S LAST SUPPER

Once upon a time, I owned a backyard swimming pool. Every spring around Mother's Day we would peel the winter cover off to reveal a funky, stagnant swamp which, through the magic of chemistry, would be transformed into sparkling, refreshing and properly chlorinated water.

Inevitably, unveiling the pool would lead to the discovery of a tiny corpse or two, hapless critters who tunneled under the tarp seeking refuge from winter's nastiness.

Moles, field mice, occasionally a chipmunk and once an exceptionally dumb bunny met their doom in the murky depths. Rubber-gloved hands removed the victims, shrouding them in supermarket plastic, then interring them in more substantial Hefties destined for landfill grave sites.

One memorable spring, we uncovered the pool to learn that an army of moles had invaded the yard. The exterminator, who commented that this was the worst mole infestation he had ever seen, stopped counting at hole #150.

These particular moles probably had degrees in engineering. Their holes were perfect circles that appeared to be drilled with precision instruments. Spaced perfectly at 2 inches apart, they surrounded the entire perimeter.

With the moles came crows. Moles are apparently gourmet fare to the crow palate, and our deck quickly became a crow sushi bar.

One crow stood out from the others. The loudest, shiniest, and undisputedly the largest, his wing span reminded me of a commuter plane. We named him Sullivan because he had that Ed Sullivan hands-behind-the back strut (OK...wings, then) and he was a "really big crow."

Sullivan, distinctive in every way, preferred to dunk his morsels in the chlorinated water as he savored them. When his meal ended, the deck lay littered with mole elbows, toes, and less tasty internal organs.

Sullivan's last supper occurred the day the exterminator powdered the holes. Using a special gizmo, he swooshed a surge of lethal mole dust down each hole and his helper, trailing with a shovel and wheelbarrow full of topsoil, quickly filled and sealed each one.

After he treated about 50 holes, the moles got the drift of what was happening. All but the suicidal ones started popping out of the yet unsealed holes, coughing and gagging.

Sullivan and his chums enjoyed a sumptuous banquet. While the moles agonized through the worst, and in most cases the last, day of their lives, the crows partied in hog heaven.

The feast lasted about an hour. Leaving mole carnage in their wake, the crows adjourned to nearby telephone poles and electric cables to celebrate their good fortune, and burp.

Sullivan, clearly a crow of breeding and culture, continued to drop by after summer showers to bathe in the warm water that collected on the laminated solar cover. Flapping his monstrous wings, he gazed longingly at the pool sides.

But the feast, sadly for him, was indeed over.

ANYTHING BUGGIN' YOU?

In my municipality, trees rule. I've seen trees hooked to life-support "IV's." Don't get me wrong; I find trees beautiful and beneficial. But I think we sometimes go over the top here with Druid-like fervor.

Until recently, a car-eating tree stood guard at the foot of my driveway. When the borough cut it down, a horde of carpenter ants became homeless.

One evening, I spied two big black ants walking side by side with more trailing behind, like two realtors leading an open house tour.

I recognized them as carpenter ants when I spotted their tiny hard hats and tool belts.

Of course, I began whacking them, and discovered at least a dozen more on my kitchen floor. Hearty critters, they required lots of squishing.

No sooner would I kill one than his buddies would pick him up and attempt to carry him away, probably to conduct some ant burial ritual.

The next day, I phoned an exterminator. They promised to dispatch a technician to assess the problem.

Rich, the Tech, arrived that afternoon and shared some fascinating facts.

He said ants SMELL water (They have NOSES? Who knew?) which is why you often find them in kitchens and bathrooms. Water, yes! I knew it wasn't my cooking that lured them.

He also explained that they're cannibals. When one dies, the others cart him off to eat him. No long-standing tradition of ant funerals; another illusion shattered.

Summers keep exterminators busy. Rich scheduled an appointment for me in a week with the actual "executioner," Earl.

Of course, I had to live through that week. I don't co-exist well with insects.

Clicking on the TV for distraction, I found a program about picnics. To keep ants from spoiling your picnic, the narrator suggested spreading talcum powder around your perimeter. Ants, with their "super-sniffers," will not cross the boundary.

I sprinted to my bathroom cabinet. In a half-hour, I created a safety-zone with my shaker of baby powder, like repelling Dracula with a cross and garlic.

Later that night, an ant approached my 50 yard line. He paused, then turned around. It worked! Hooray!

Earl came a week later and did a wonderful job. I'd been enjoying a pest-free summer since, until last weekend.

My friend Lorraine visited and discovered a water leak in my basement. That night, we found two ants on the kitchen counter.

If water attracts ants, I had Myrtle Beach in my cellar. I pictured swarms frolicking with sun glasses, surfboards (Hang 6 !), and Margaritas.

I phoned the company again.

"This is my second call this summer," I began. "I guess that makes me a 'frequent flier,' or in this case...'crawler'!"

Earl returned, as guaranteed.

I also called my plumber, who fixed the leak. Water stopped; problem solved; beach closed!

So, is anything buggin' you?

PHIL TO ATTEND FIRST ANNUAL GROUNDHOG'S DAY MUSIC FESTIVAL

Johnstown celebrates music. We honor history (Windber Coal Miners); ethnic traditions (Polka Fest, Ethnic Fest); agriculture (Ebensburg Potato Fest); even "hot" technology (Thunder in the Valley).

But our eclectic mix of music adds spirit and revelry to every event. We are one rhythmic, harmonized, tuneful, toe-tapping town.

Many celebrations occur in warmer months. We need a winter gala, an opportunity to fete a Pennsylvania icon, an enduring folklore figure…Punxsutawney Phil.

His legendary weather predictions rank him among the nation's top prognosticators. Joe DeNardo, Al Roker, and Tony Martin all respect his skill.

Phil's cousin, Alexander Graham Groundhog, founded the Punxsutawney Branch of the Smithsonian Planetarium, linking Phil to The Weather Channel 24/7.

The humble rodent who launched his career in 1906 at Gobbler's Knob was knighted by Queen Elizabeth as Lord High Weather Commissioner. Ronald Reagan welcomed Phil to the White House. In 1993, Phil starred in his own major motion picture.

Norman Chynoweth of Benscreek, a loyal Phil follower, has amassed a mind-boggling collection of groundhog memorabilia. A cross between a diorama and a model train set, his museum-quality display captures the history and tradition, as well as the mystique and mischievous nature of His Majesty High Hogness.

Norman's dedication caught Phil's attention. Although he is deluged by requests for personal appearances, Phil announced he will leave Gobbler's Knob as soon as the ceremony ends, and journey the 67 miles to Johnstown.

Norman, an accomplished musician, is scheduled to appear with his group, "Cajun Norm and the Jam Session Band," at Wooly's Celtic Bar and Grill, Feb. 2nd and 3rd.

Phil will host the First Annual Groundhog's Day Music Festival. Norman will be titled "High Groundhog History Ambassador."

As a journalist, I confirmed this news in a phone conversation with Phil himself.

"I'm delighted to speak to you, Your Highness. I understand 30,000 fans journeyed to Gobbler's Knob last year. You draw crowds like a rock star!"

"Yes, I'm proud to say my career is soaring. Not bad for a critter who lives in a burrow. But my 'hibernaculum'…that's what I call it, has a Craftmatic bed, a big screen TV and a clapper."

"Wow!" I replied. "How will you travel?"

"I bought one of Willie Nelson's old tour buses. A palace on wheels. I need to get out of Punxy a bit more. When I heard about Norman's collection, I KNEW I had to see it in person. Plus, Johnstown's music festivals are getting well-known. Great reviews."

"I have a photo of you, Phil. You look great for 111."

"Oil of Olay Regenerist," he confided. "And L'Oreal is great for fur."

"Could I have your paw-tograph?"

"Certainly, honey," he laughed. "See ya in two weeks."

Wow! Phil's Music Festival at Wooly's. I'll be there both nights! Join me. I wonder if Norman knows "Muskrat Love?" I've heard him play "Wild Thing" and "Rocky Raccoon."

We're covered.

CHAPTER 7: BON APPETIT

GADD ZUKES

"I've had fresh veggies from my garden all summer!"galpal Jennifer declared proudly. "From my garden to the table."

Green thumb Cathie announced "Stuffed peppers and halupki for Labor Day!"

"I'm trying a great new pumpkin pie recipe," promised my sister-in-law Lisa.

I respect these resourceful ladies and their agricultural and kitchen creativity. I'm NOT one of them! You might say I'm "culinarily challenged."(You also might say Hannibal Lechter had an eating disorder.

I'm a non-cultivator and a non-epicurian; can't grow it, can't cook it. A fine line separates "melts in your mouth" from "decomposition." I've crossed it more than once.

My sausage-flavored chocolate chip cookies taught me an important lesson: clean the broiler before you bake.

Holiday meals that other women whip up effortlessly defeat me. Usually recognizable seasonal fare has emerged from my oven looking like weasel intestines.

Another sister-in-law suggested that I watch the Food Network to learn from Rachael and Emeril. I tuned in just as Paula Deen was about to tell us what to do with okra. I know what to do with okra.

One frigid winter night, my then-husband dragged home from work, chilled and exhausted.

"Today couldn't have gone worse," he groaned, plopping down at the dinner table.

"Wait." I plunked his plate on the table. "It's NOT over yet."

New recipe (from a 50 cent cookbook purchased at a yard sale)- macaroni and brie cheese. It sounded elegant to me. Alas, it looked like vomit and smelled like gym socks.

.Al and Jean, a precious elderly couple, lived in my 'hood in the 80's and 90's. Every spring they planted an amazing garden which, by August and September, yielded a bounty of delicious vegetables. They always shared.

One afternoon, Jean knocked at my door with zucchini bread, a delicacy I had never tasted.

Despite being legally blind, Jean managed to prepare many savory goodies. The bread was awesome. I asked for her recipe.

That night, I did some nocturnal baking to avoid the daytime heat. Following her instructions, I popped a loaf pan of the zucchini mixture into my Tappan and salivated, as I awaiting the finished product...warm, succulent zucchini bread. Yum!

(Ok, you know where this is headed. Work with me.)

When 45 minutes at 350 had passed, I flung the oven door open to and discovered ...a pan of disgusting blackened glop.

The gunk a mechanic scraped from the crankcase of my dad's old Desoto had looked more appetizing. I stuck it in the fridge.

At 10 am, I rapped at Jean's door, glop in one hand and recipe in the other.

"Jean," I wailed, " I followed your instructions to the letter! What went wrong?"

She sat down and reached for her special lighted magnifying gizmo. She frowned at the glop, then perused the recipe. A minute later, her laughter shook the house.

"Oh, Michele, I'm so sorry. I forgot to write down '2 cups of flour.'"

We both howled. It was clearly a case of the legally blind leading the legally blond.

Some folks have eaten at my house and gone on to live healthy, normal lives. But I don't push my luck.

The only reason I have a kitchen is because it came with the apartment.

IT'S HARD TO ZEST A PLASTIC LEMON

At Thanksgiving, we count our blessings and express gratitude. You readers can be thankful that I've never invited you to dinner.

Some folks have eaten at my house and gone on to live healthy, normal lives. Others, however, tell frightening tales of grisly inedibility. Savory and usually recognizable holiday dishes have emerged looking like weasel intestines and tasting worse.

If you listen carefully, you can hear a terrified gasp when I steer my shopping cart down the turkey aisle. Fresh or frozen, these birds know the meaning of "cruel and unusual punishment."

Years ago, my friend Marlene offered me advice. "If you can read, you can cook."

I can read, honest! I just fumble techniques, misuse ingredients, lose track of time…you get the idea.

For years, I dodged the dreaded turkey preparation bullet, relying on family to feed me. But in 1979, I decided to tackle a Butterball. I purchased a tinfoil roaster, cans of corn and green beans, two boxes of Stove Top Stuffing, a jumbo canister of Potato Buds, and four jars of Heinz gravy.

When the turkey was done, I discovered I'd made a classic "first bird" error. Two crispy paper baggies of giblets and gizzards crinkled in his cavity.

My mother-in-law baked pies. My mom brought festive napkins, serving plates, and her special green damask tablecloth.

Hubby fired up the electric knife and began to carve…THROUGH the tinfoil roaster, ON the tablecloth. Juices saturated the damask and dripped on the linoleum..

One season, I attempted fudge. I was short one cup of sugar, but rationalized "So what? Fudge is sweet enough."

Sugar helps fudge "clot."

It didn't help when I hastily selected the wrong little brown bottle from the cupboard, adding 2 teaspoons of Gravy Master instead of vanilla.

Somewhere on a landfill, that fudge is still moving!

My guests must have low expectations and even lower standards.

I prepared my most infamous turkey in 2005. Galpal Denise suggested I buy a boneless turkey breast and simply cook it in my crockpot. Foolproof, right?

I unwrapped the 7 lb breast. The shiny skin appeared to be covered with lines. It looked…well…quilted. I Pam-sprayed the crock and bird, added a can of chicken broth, and set the dial.

I'd invited only 5 guests. One of the guys lifted the thing from the pot and readied the Sunbeam knife to carve. Then, he started laughing, uncontrollably!

The "shiny skin" was actually an additional layer of plastic covering. The "quilting" came from the twine that bound the tender meat securely.

"Look!" my buddy exclaimed. "An S & M turkey!"

My friends still recall "Michele's Bondage Bird."

This year, I made what I make best: reservations!

THE TRUTH ABOUT BLACK FRIDAY

Thanksgiving passed. I hope all of you remembered to set your scales back 10 lbs last Wednesday night.

Is it me, or were the Black Friday advertisements particularly aggressive, persistent and annoying this season?

I have no memory of Black Friday shopping expeditions from my childhood. I realize now the BF experience started in 1961, in a place my mom would know how (and why) to avoid. Read on.

Remember the "Blue Laws," legislation designed to restrict or ban retail activity on Sundays and holidays for religious reasons? I thought we didn't shop on those days because nothing was open!

So, I looked it up. Most Blue Laws have been challenged (and lost) constitutionally. But (check THIS out) in Massachusetts, Maine, and Rhode island, retail and grocery stores MUST remain closed on Thanksgiving and Christmas!

The word "doorbuster" conjures up images of impatient crowds growing crazed and hostile. In 2008, unruly shoppers waited for an upstate New York Walmart 's 5 a.m. opening. Becoming a frenzied mob, they broke down the huge glass door and squished a 34 year old "greeter," killing him.

Reports from the scene described stampeding customers stepping around, even hopping over, the dead body. Doorbuster? You betcha!

Only in America would folks trample each other over "sales" exactly 1 day after claiming to be thankful for what they already have.

John Wayne once said, "Life is hard. It's even harder if you're stupid."

Folks believe the name "Black Friday" indicates the point in bookkeeping when retailers can declare their profits "in the black" (as opposed to "in the red").

Wrong! That may apply, but in 1961, Philadelphia police coined the BF phrase to call attention to an escalating problem. Heavy traffic and disruptive pedestrians clogged roadways and crosswalks. Officers observed citizens pushing, shoving, and threatening one another while shopping. Violence erupted when some customers brandished guns and knives.

Yeah, yeah, blame Philadelphia! But remember, Philly gave us the Declaration of Independence, cheese-steak sandwiches, and Fabian.

I COULDN'T MAKE THIS UP! (I would have said "Jersey.") Type "Black Friday History" into your browser and see what turns up.

I saw a poster showing an angry, red-faced Santa exclaiming, "Slow down! Let's eat the #$&@ turkey first!"

Meanwhile, civilized folks tuned their TV's to watch the President pardon the "National Turkey."

We gobbled; we burped; some of us shopped. Now it's time to decorate the house and trim the tree.

I thanked God for rescuing me from health problems, blessing me with a loving family and caring friends, and giving me a talent that makes others smile.

If you ask me, there are a lot of turkeys out there who need to be pardoned.

DISSIN' HOLIDAY FOODS

Recently, I asked readers what traditional holiday dish, prepared by Grammas, aunts, etc, do they miss. Responses flooded in, a touching homage to a tranquil, more innocent era.

Now, let's get NASTY! With one mega-meal to go, plus maybe 3 or 4 parties, I predict you'll spot one dish so revolting that your horrified intestines will plead for mercy.

What sickens me? Glad you asked.

CHEESE BALLS. A port-wine cheeseball looks like curdled bloody brain matter. It's probably a mixture of Velveeta processed cheese (and *what is PROCESSED CHEESE?*) and 2 bottles of "Mad Dog." Guests are expected to smear a glob on a cracker...*crunch!*

FRUITCAKES ...are approaching long deserved extinction. Unpopular fruit wedges are marinated in the booze of one's choice, then combined with embalming-quality preservatives, guaranteeing the dessert will have the texture of an L. L. Bean work boot.

Johnny Carson believed there is only 1 fruitcake in the world, and its weapons-grade coating enables perpetual re-gifting.

SWEET POTATOES and/or YAMS. As kids, we craved s'mores and Swiss Miss cocoa topped with mini-marshmallows. Face it; If Mom melted marshmallows on compost, we'd have eaten it.

"Hey! Where's the sweet potato casserole?"

ASPIC. When I was 8, I loved tomato juice. Mom, who had a devious streak, wanted me to eat more vegetables. Tomato juice and unflavored Knox gelatin formed the base for aspic.

Cooks hastily tossed in anything...olives, strawberries, Barbie high heels, green pepper chunks, beets, Legos....you see, aspic's flaw was a time constraint.

"C'mon," called Mom, "the aspic's gelled." (CLOTTED)

GREEN BEAN CASSEROLE. Green bean casserole started as a

Lenten side dish, basically green beans, noodles, and cream of mushroom soup. I loved it.

When I became an Atkins dieter, I re-designed it. The green beans and mushroom soup remained, but the noodles were out. I added 1 can drained tuna fish, 1 jar sliced mushrooms, and topped it with surprisingly lo-carb French's French-fried onions, crushed.

On a whim, I sent the recipe off to a women's magazine and won 1st prize.

Then I went to a party and discovered a shameful, hybrid version of my masterpiece on a buffet table. The green beans stayed but the noodles were back. The tuna, sliced mushrooms, and mushroom soup had vanished.

I scooped a taste. Green beans topped with French's onion bits floated…FLOATED…on an ocean of white scum that tasted like horseradish and Oil of Olay, a squeeze of Pepsodent and a pinch of Sakrete.

Our smiling hostess twirled by. "The secret's in the sauce," she giggled, echoing "Sipsey" (think" Fried Green Tomatoes.") I wanted to hurt someone.

CRANBERRY SAUCE. Another party, another buffet line.

"I hate this rancid, jiggling stuff," a man hissed to his wife (except he didn't say "stuff.")

I'd finally found another human who disses cranberry sauce. I hate to be in the same room with it.

Folks describe "corn on the cob" as "edible summer." Cranberry sauce is congealed, twitching evil. I hear that it's made by mixing cherry jello, scraple, an eyeball, and Howdy Doody in a Ninja Blender.

Just sayin'…

So, worried about a few extra pounds creeping on this month? Cut this out, keep it handy, read it before dinner on the 25th and before any parties. You might even lose a little.

CHAPTER 8: ON MY OWN

GLASS DOORKNOBS AND CASEMENT WINDOWS

The first house I remember living in had casement windows and glass door knobs.

Those windows seemed like doors to me. I'd crank one open, savor floral fragrances, listen to crickets, and watch lightening bugs. Hello, World!

Hey, I was 3.

Some twenty years later, I chatted with a real estate lady. "I like classic touches."

"I know just the place," she smiled.

Standing out front, she pointed across the street. "That's the Oakland Fire Hall. They hold a giant Fireman's Jubilee every spring."

I flashed back to age 9, sitting in my dad's Pontiac, stopped at the light in the Oakland section of town. I heard the music, smelled the food, and yearned to ride the Ferris wheel, aglow with brilliant neon against the night sky.

I fantasized about spinning on the swings, or tossing a ring to win a silly plastic prize.

"Sold!" I declared.

Did I mention the casement windows and glass door knobs? I spent eleven special years in a neighborhood where warm, friendly people cared about and helped one another.

We had 1 traffic light, 2 playgrounds with tennis courts, 2 gas stations, and 2 bars. Many work mornings, I sleepily applied lipstick at the light. I attempted tennis, but me whacking at that ball was like a rabbit trying to play a violin.

I shared my home with my loving Irish Setter, Bridget. We walked daily and met fascinating folks. Oaklanders maintained their houses and tended their gardens. Neighbors waved, and we waved and wagged back.

I never slept the night before a festival. I'd crank my casements wide and listen to workers unloading trucks, assembling rides and constructing shelves.

Neighbors, friends and firemen supervised booths, games, and food preparation. Carnival workers operated the rides. Music played. Crowds sampled the foods. Folks played games, enjoyed rides, and celebrated the season.

The inconvenience of cars parked everywhere annoyed some residents, but most rolled with it.

A man with a Chrysler full of children became stuck in a drainage ditch in front of my house (I called it my "moat."). Instead of phoning AAA, I hopped in their car, straightened the front wheels, and eased that dinosaur out.

The night of the '77 Flood, Bridget and I huddled on the rug by the front door. The power and phone were gone, and water rose in my basement.

The house caught fire when lightning struck the second floor, but the torrential rain extinguished the flames.

The next afternoon, a group of guys brought a ladder, tools, and a huge tarp to cover the gaping hole in my siding.

It was ok.

We were family.

And every spring we shared jubilee magic. It swept the bad stuff away.

I never slept closing night either. I still opened the casements wide, even turning the glass door knob of the spare room to achieve "stereo."

It saddened me to hear the "tear-down" and the packing. But it reminded me that, more than likely, the best of summer lay ahead.

GROOVIEST HOUSE ON THE BLOCK

Olbum's Furniture Store fascinated my mom much like jewelry mesmerized Audrey Hepburn in the movie "Breakfast at Tiffany's." Both stores sold high-end merchandise and, for the most part, neither Mom nor Audrey could afford it.

But Mom saved and purchased a pair of club chairs from Olbum's. She liked Penn Furniture, too, and bought a curved green velvet sofa from them.

Time marched on. Prestigious stores that catered to wealthier clientele faded away.

Friends who know me well will tell you that all my taste is in my mouth. I spent the 60's watching the Partridge Family, James Bond and Ann Margaret movies, and Laugh-In, which prepared me to furnish my first house. It would be the trendiest, "grooviest" house in Johnstown.

I bought a little two-bedroom Cape Cod from the original owners. They were moving to an apartment, and had never changed a thing since the house was built in 1936.

Gee Bee Discount Furniture (in *my price range*) had a living room display in their window that left me breathless: A black "fur" sofa, matching chair, and 2-person size chaise lounge, accented by a chrome and glass coffee table and end tables. (I bought Windex in 55 gallon drums for 12 years, but it was WORTH it!).

While I filled out credit forms, I spotted a roll of brilliant red SHAG carpet. Perfect.

At another store, I purchased 2 red ginger jar lamps and a red accent chair. Fairly good at sewing, I made drapes (NOT CURTAINS! Drapes, with tape and all!) out of black and white print fabric from Penneys.

I purchased a plain beige dinette with a brown tabletop. The 6 chairs had beige frames but freaky brown naughahyde seats. I predict there will be no retro-comeback for that quirky mutant fabric. Naughas challenged hunters from the start, but once the frisky animals heard DISCO they became impossible to trap.

The bathroom was my masterpiece. It came with lavender fixtures...HONEST! A lavender tub, commode, and pedestal sink were surrounded by white wainscoting (fake wood tile) and a white chair rail.

I bought lavender paint at the hardware store and began to create.

Alas, it was waaay too much lavender, as if Tinkerbell imploded in Barbie's Dream House.

I was working in an old bright orange t-shirt. I realized it looked great next to the sink. Hmmm…orange walls? But what about the chair rail? I opened the medicine cabinet, and a tube of hot pink lipstick rolled out . An omen? I thought so. I took the shirt and lipstick to the hardware.

The finished product amazed family and friends. Lavender fixtures, orange walls, and hot pink chair rail…maybe "amazed" isn't quite the word.

I knew I reached perfection when my mom walked in one day and shrieked, "WHAT have you done to this house?"

I could almost hear Tommy James singing "Crimson and Clover."

Yes, the 70's gave us flocked wallpaper, KISS, Hugo's, and Joann Worley.

45 years later, we have Smart Cars, Minions, Smart Phones, and NKOTB (New Kids On The Block) who are in their mid to late 40's.

The 70's are baaack. Find your mood ring and roll with it.

IN A GROOVY MOOD

Apparently, in the 70's, my house wasn't the trendiest or "grooviest."

What a shock! Friends and readers deluged me with descriptions of their horrific décor in response to my Aug. 23 column, "Roll with the 70's."

"Alien" green was a popular living room color.

"I had an olive green sofa and glass-top end tables with gold carved legs and feet," wrote my friend Carm. "I also painted my bathroom *brown* and bought orange and white plaid shower and window curtains from Penney's."

Sharon from Harrisburg recalled her green faux fur sofa, and the kitchen that she painted orange.

"When I read about your lavender, pink and orange bathroom, I thought of my first apartment with a claw foot bathtub," E'd reader Debbie. "I spent one whole weekend painting it yellow."

Friends shouldn't let friends drink and paint.

70's folks appeared to love furniture and bathtubs with feet, another trend I must have missed. Personally, I want my tub and furnishings to stand absolutely still! I'd be really upset if I caught an end table trying to sneak out the back door.

My pal Jane described her dinette set. "I had a glass-top table, of course, and barrel chairs made of coated wire on pedestals. "

I remember those chairs. The backs and seats were like a playground fence. When I stood up, my dupa looked like I'd been sitting on a vegematic.

"Hurrah for naugahyde and hot pink lipstick!" cheered Lorraine from Reading.

"I used a 10 x 12 precut piece of lattice as a room divider," confessed reader Louise. "I cursed it every week when I had to dust it!"

I'm not a "duster." I believe dust was created to measure time. I don't like to mess with history.

"I still have my mood ring," laughed my friend Jere from Florida. "And I had an orange beaded 'curtain' hanging in a doorway."

"Do you still have it?" I asked. "I have an open pantry in my kitchen. That would be PERFECT!"

The 60's and 70's celebrated the Beach Boys, the Righteous Brothers, muscle cars, madras, Woodstock, Kojak, and the Moon landing.

I love that I get to relive some of the magic.

Pixie haircuts (think Twiggy) have returned. Maxi dresses are back (varicose vein camouflage!). And I hear that this fall a new Shelby Cobra will be introduced.

It doesn't get better than that.

As I finish typing this, Jere in Neptune Beach is searching her attic for that curtain.

CHECKMATE

I loved teaching at Johnstown Vo-Tech.

Geniuses in education put vocational skills, technical training, and academics under one roof, and invited seven districts to send students there. The diversity created magic.

City kids mixed with rural kids, jocks with geeks, future workers with bookworms, in a melting pot of ethnicity. It delighted me to take part in such an innovative approach to learning.

I was 22. My problem, insisted some of my colleagues, stemmed from being a person first and a teacher after that. Many of them believed the warning handed down from generations of educators: "Don't smile till Christmas."

I wanted success for my students, but I cared more about the people they would become than scores on a test. I took Algebra (at gunpoint) in 9th grade and never used it yet!

Time travel with me to 1972. Vo-Tech, in its second year of operation, had a chess club. Ten guys met weekly with a male advisor in his classroom.

But, in early February, the teacher quit. Rumor said he'd received a more lucrative offer elsewhere. Unfortunately, his departure spawned 10 chess-playing "orphans."

No advisor, no club. These fellas spent 6 months perfecting their techniques. Their goal, to enter a city wide tournament in May, swirled in the "bowl."

I know nothing about chess.

"I don't know a pawn from a bingo marker!" I explained.

"We'll behave," they assured me. "We just need a warm teacher body in the room."

OK, body with pulse...I could do that. But I didn't have a classroom. I "traveled," the administration called it. Every class period when the bell rang, I gathered my stuff and changed rooms like the kids. (I remained "roomless" for 8 years.)

When I presented our plight to the principal, he offered us a small conference room at the rear of the main office.

April came quickly. The entry fee for the competition was $50. For high school boys in '72, that was like $500.

We got permission to hold a bake sale one afternoon in the hall outside the cafeteria. While "chess moms" and girlfriends fired up ovens to supply goodies, our guys papered the walls with posters reading, "Help the Chess Club get out of the office and into the Tournament."

And then, May arrived.

My mother and I fought over every stitch of clothing I wore from the day I left the playpen. I dressed 70's style... sort of Bohemian on steroids. That wouldn't fly with conservative chess judges.

I knew she'd dress me "prim and proper." She loaned me a gray pencil-skirt suit, then added a high-necked white blouse and "sensible" low-heeled pumps.

In 1972, I could sit on my hair. I ironed it in a futile attempt to look like Cher. It made Mom crazy. We swept it up and used 800 bobby pins to fashion a tight, pristine "bun." I looked like the love child of Miss Grundy (think Archie comics) and Janet Reno.

The hushed atmosphere at the library fed my anxiety. I didn't know whether to scratch my watch or wind my fanny. I mimicked the other advisors, strolling about and pausing at tables to whisper "Smart move, Richard," or similar encouragement.

44 years later, I don't remember whether we won or lost. In the end, it didn't matter. We bonded and accomplished a goal.

When a teacher learns a life lesson, that's what really counts.

HIBERNATION

I Love Hibernation

Autumn clocked in slowly this year. September treated us to 14 days with temps between 75 and 83 degrees. October gave us 11 of them. I loved it!

But signs of fall inched along. The birds disappeared. Trees shed leaves. Animals behaved strangely.

My neighbor Marlene decorated her patio using gourds and pumpkins. The next day, it was ravaged. Paw prints marked the crime scene.

One morning at dawn, I thought I spotted a squirrel pushing a wheelbarrow full of nuts across our parking lot, but I could have been wrong.

I hate cold and dark. Snow and ice scare me. I understand hibernation. When the sun sets at 4:30, I could eat dinner, put my jammies on, and call it a day.

This week Mother Nature really rubbed our noses in it. Sunday we turned the clocks back. (Wise folks also turned their scales back 10 lbs or so. Holiday Goodies Alert!) Tuesday, big wet snowflakes advertised coming attractions. If that was the commercial, I don't wanna see the show!

Woolly worms are terrorizing folklore believers. People glimpsed totally black fuzzies scurrying for shelter, allegedly a bad omen.

I looked it up. Woolly worms and groundhogs have minimal skill as meteorologists.

I'm ready for spring by January 2. February 1, I'm usually so sick of winter that I could stuff and roast Phil before he gets his chance to forecast.

Eastern gray squirrels live in trees. They stock up on nuts at Sam's Club, insulate their nests with leaves and compost, and snuggle with their families. My friend Sharon in Harrisburg once shared her yard with a squirrel family. Earl Squirrel and his wife, Girl Squirrel, fascinated us with their antics.

Two houses ago, I met an extraordinary chipmunk. I named him Floyd. He lived in a vacant garage on our alley; no underground burrow for him. Fearless, he scampered down my deck daily to observe us humans.

Since it's customary to offer food to company, I served peanuts. From a handful, he packed 5 nuts snugly in his pudgy cheeks (5 is apparently chipmunk cheek capacity). He'd dash home, fill his cupboard, and return for the rest.

He became "family." 5:30 pm was dinnertime. Floyd dropped by and loaded up. If I ran late, he'd pose on his hind legs, "hands" on his tiny hips, and chatter angrily at the back door.

He had a temper. One afternoon he caught another chipmunk filching his stash. Floyd kicked rodent butt that day, a miniature Rocky Balboa.

After two seasons, Floyd disappeared. I fear that something he disagreed with ate him.

Hibernation rocks. When you're dormant, underground or in a cozy tree, you don't miss light. Humans miss light.

I hate diseases, natural catastrophes, war, man's inhumanity to man, and daylight savings time.

December 21 marks the winter solstice. We are allotted 9 hours and 17 minutes of light. Two days later, we get 9 hours and 18 minutes. Yes, light increases by 30 seconds per day.

But things perk up. On March 21, the first day of spring, we bask in 12 hours and 13 minutes of (hopefully) sunlight!

Only 127 days to go. (Sigh)

I swear I just saw a bear drive by in a Ford F150. The bed was jam packed with rolls of Charmin. But I could be wrong.

WITCH AND FAMOUS

Lon Chaney, Bela Lugosi, and Boris Karloff pioneered '30's and '40's horror films. However, the turbulent, reckless spirit of the '60's led movie producers to seek new boundaries. Cinema historians dubbed that period the "Golden Age of Horror."

Baby boomers packed drive-ins to see Hitchcock flicks ("Psycho," "The Birds") and William Castle classics ("Thirteen Ghosts," "Rosemary's Baby"). Vincent Price movies ("The Pit and the Pendulum," "The House of Usher") introduced Edgar Allen Poe's graphic literature to teens who knew the depraved genius only by Cliff Notes.

Possibly the most zealous innovator, George Romero, reigned as "Father of the Zombie Genre." A Carnegie Mellon graduate, Romero adopted Pittsburgh as his home. "Night of the Living Dead," filmed in a rural Pittsburgh location in '68, set a new standard for shocking zombie carnage.

I taught English, writing in particular. I knew how to break language components down so my students' words would take them where they wanted to go.

Motivating them and stimulating their imaginations was something else, much like trying to show a moose how to tango.

Generations of students began school years writing "How I Spent My Sumer Vacation." I wanted to raise the bar and offer trendy essay topics. I decided to tap into this youthful fascination with horror and the occult.

A campy article in an old magazine suggested "Do-It-Yourself Palm Reading…Discover Your Future!" It included a hand diagram and a list of what the variations in lines and wrinkles meant. I made copies and passed them out.

"How cool is this?" I thought. I anticipated themes full of insight, self-awareness, maybe even self-discovery.

I got a bunch of teens examining their hands as if they'd never seen them before.

"Which one's my index finger?"
"Do thumbs count?"
"I think my pinky is double-jointed!"
"No, that's *not* your heart line. It's ditto ink."
Tireless innovator, I tried Plan B.

The '60's horror craze incited rumors of alleged spook sightings and supernatural occurrences. I drove (in daytime) to 3 popular locations that I deemed harmless, and took photos. I designed a bulletin board using the pix and descriptive blurbs, calling it "The Local Haunts."

The assignment: Select a spot and write about an imaginary adventure you had there.

I did not *say* "Visit!" Unfortunately, classes organized "unofficial field trips" and descended on the sites like crows on roadkill.

Some scoured the woods by the Incline Plane searching for the ghostly coal miner killed in a 1902 explosion.

Others visited Forest Lawn Cemetery hoping for a glimpse of a mysterious female apparition wearing a white gown.

The majority trekked to "Becky's Grave." This attraction occupied a remote corner of a private family graveyard just outside Elton. It was simply an empty hole where a casket had been removed and likely relocated. But gossip abounded.

Legend claimed that Becky befriended an Indian who reciprocated by teaching her "medicine man crafts." Villagers discovered her tending a pot of magic potion. They labeled her a witch and executed her.

In 1996, I "un-retired" for financial reasons. "Subbing" is the dregs of education employment. Gigs could last a day, weeks, or months, and not everyone was a "satisfied customer."

Too frequently, I encountered students whose parents I taught 20 years earlier.

One afternoon, a student innocently raised her hand. "Are you a witch?"

"If that was true, you'd all be toads," I replied.

She was relentless. "My mom says you're a witch."

"As I recall, your mom had trouble with spelling."

Clearly, Becky had returned to bite me on the dupa for unleashing teenagers who interrupted her slumbers.

It's true: If you can't stir with the big girls, step away from the cauldron!.

CAN WE TALK?

I think," observed the weatherman, "our hottest days are behind us."
"NO!" I wailed.
Some folks are okay with summer's end. NOT ME!
For shy, modest, insecure ladies, swimwear season has passed.
At 12, I needed a "grown-up" suit. Rosemarie Reids were too adult, and Catalinas were too expensive. I settled on a pink-flowered Jantzen.

I recall these swimsuit memories vividly because 2 significant, noteworthy events occurred this summer distracting us from pesky hurricanes, serial killers, plane crashes, tornados, government scandals and outrageous behavior by celebrities.

What 2 incidents, you ask?

Esther Williams died. Joan Rivers didn't.

Esther gained prominence in the mid-1930's. An attractive, athletic young woman with Olympic-caliber skills, she developed into a serious aquatic competitor. Unfortunately, World War II prevented her from participating in the 1940 Olympics.

Hollywood, however, quickly recognized a new and rare talent to exploit. Esther starred in a succession of mediocre films. Moviegoers flocked to them.

Esther always played a professional swimmer. Lavish underwater photography wowed audiences, and Esther's wholesome personality and unpretentious manner won her the respect of her fans.

She died June 6 at 91.

Joan Rivers celebrated her 80th birthday June 8.

She began her career as a comedienne, but as talk shows evolved, Joan found a niche.

Joan is one of the most morally reprehensible entertainers of our time. A narcissistic personality, she fancies herself a fashion icon. She regularly maligns celebrities clothing, casual and formal, with obscene, scathing comments, mostly unwarranted.

Granted, many famous artists select costumes that even Honey Boo Boo would reject.

When Elizabeth Taylor was alive (God Rest her Soul), Joan made her life a nightmare, scrutinizing every item she wore and every ounce she gained or lost.

When Joan went too far, she relied on "damage control."

"We really LOVE you, Liz," she'd hiss. "Take better care of yourself."

At 80, Joan surrounds herself with a cluster of toadies who echo her opinions no matter what.

Summers bring out the worst in her. Vulgar, crude, bathing suit critiques spew from her forked tongue.

Esther, who spent her retirement years designing flattering yet practical swimwear styles, dismissed today's extreme erotic trends.

"Two Dixie cups strung together with fishing wire is NOT a bathing suit," she declared.

Joan continues to work, steering her "Fashion Police" program to new lows. She occasionally visits New York for special celebrations, but lives primarily in Malibu, California.

Joan, can we talk? Piranhas swim in that water. So do squid and jellyfish.

Be a sport, Joan. Stay out of the surf. Give the piranhas a breather.

CHAPTER 9: LICORICE SPEAKS

LICORICE LENDS A PAW

Hello. I bet you expected Michele Bender's column to appear here today. Michele had an operation, so I'm taking her place this week.

Her doctor removed something called "cataracts" from her eyes. It figures! Anything having to do with CATS can't POSSIBLY be good!

I guess by now you've noticed, I'm a dog. My name is Licorice. I take care of Joe, a human, one of Michele's friends.

I'm a Scottish terrier. Michele says I have "attitude." I'm not sure what that is, but I think I like it.

People have a lot of misconceptions about dogs. For instance, many of us can read and write. We just do it covertly so humans won't feel threatened.

If I had longer legs, I know I could drive Joe's truck, too. But I love to ride in it.

And television fascinates me. Every time another dog, cat or animal comes on the screen, I do my best to jump up and capture it. So far, I've been unsuccessful.

As long as I'm revealing canine secrets, we dogs can also talk. All humans hear is "Arf," or "Bow-wow," or "Woof." Those sounds actually comprise "Dogspeak," our language.

Of course, there are dialects. German shepherds communicate differently than French poodles. But we get each other's drift. Humans would be amazed by what their dogs say about them.

I love to go for walks. Sometimes Joe and I follow paths through the woods in where Joe and I live. There are loads of nifty sights and smells.

When we visit Michele's house, I like to walk Joe on the sidewalk. It's a change from the woods, and I get to poke and sniff a different variety of stuff.

A handsome pug lives up the street from Michele's house. Usually, he woofs admiringly when we pass. Of course, I play "hard to get," and simply sashay on by.

The last time we met the pug, he went ballistic on me, lunging and growling for no reason. He barked some very nasty things. When I walk Joe on the sidewalk again, I plan to give that critter a piece of my mind.

Even though we're about the same size, I could kick his tail around the block with three paws tied behind my back! What nerve!

Speaking of walks and sidewalks, I want to remind you humans that we dogs aren't as tall as you folks. My legs only measure 8 inches. That puts my fur-covered body very close to steaming, scorching concrete and asphalt surfaces.

Extreme heat like we've been having calls for extra care. Shorter walks during cooler hours would help. Maybe carry a bottle of water, too. And remember, NEVER leave us locked in a hot car!

Now that Michele's doctor removed those "cat things" from her eyes, I know she'll be back writing for you soon. But "subbing" for her has really been fun.

Wags and woofs to all!

LICORICE CASTS HER VOTE

Hello, again. Michele Bender's column usually appears here.

For you first-timers, I'm Licorice, a 6 year old Scottish terrier. My pet human, Joe, is a friend of Michele's. I've "subbed" for her before in emergencies, but you'll be pleased to know that she's not sad, stressed, or having yet another worn-out part replaced.(Humans aren't very durable.).

I'm writing today because I had amazing experiences I wanted to share.

For one thing, Michele and I had a serious chat. She has a habit of calling me "Baby." It worked in the movie "Dirty Dancing," but it doesn't work for me.

I told her, "Girlfriend, I've grown up. I'm 6 now. Thanks to you, I'm a popular local columnist and, as a 'terrier activist', I woof loudly concerning animal abuse and neglect."

"Lic, I totally respect you," she replied. "Can I call you 'sweetheart'?"

"Fine," I nodded.

My most rewarding adventure occurred just last week. I VOTED! Joe took me with him to our local precinct.

Voting is serious business, and I wanted my first time to count. One lady marked my paw print in her book. I presented my license as ID.

I selected candidates who I believe will improve schools, and crack down on criminals, especially abusers of ANY SORT!

As we left the building, something magical happened. Probably the most handsome, dignified, and...yes, sexy...black Scotty I ever saw stood in the parking lot.

He noticed me, too. He gently nudged his human in my direction. I learned his name is Tavish McDuff and his pet human was one of the election ladies. Her neighbor walked him over to visit while she voted.

"Mac" (I call him "Mac") and I sniffed each other thoroughly. He left me breathless. I'm a pushover for "Hartz Mountain."

He told me he'll turn 10 on December 15. I adore older men! If he has a party, I hope he invites me. Sparks flew, let me tell you!

December (sigh) and winter lurk right around the corner. I want to remind you humans that canine needs change seasonally. Keep us with you in your warm homes. Bundle us in coats and sweaters when we go out.

Rinse the salt off our paws when we come back inside. Salt feels icky, and the temptation to lick it off is irresistible. It can irritate our feets, and make us ill if we swallow it.

Parasites (fleas, ticks, and worse) seek out warm, healthy dogs and cats for winter "lodging." Urge your human to keep you immunized all year long.

Dear humans, care for us the way we care for you!

And "Mac," if you read this, Happy Birthday, Baby!

LICORICE TO THE RESCUE

Hello, again. Michele Bender's column usually appears here, but I dig in and help when I can. I'm Licorice, a Scottish terrier. My pet human, Joe, is a pal of Michele's.

Friday morning, March 5, our phone rang early. Joe grabbed my leash. "We've gotta get to Michele's," Joe explained. I smelled trouble.

When we arrived, Michele was sitting on her floor, crying. I dashed over and gave her a huge "poochie-moochie," but it didn't help.

She told us she fainted and fell on the floor. She said she'd been dizzy and sick all week because she had a bug.

I understand bugs. I had fleas once, and ticks three different times. Bugs make animals and humans miserable.

I supervised while Joe and our friend Leanne wheelchaired Michele to the car. I hugged her until Joe dropped me off at home. He then took her to the hospital, but I made him promise to call as soon as he had news.

Doctors had to give her a brand new right hip, and she broke her left toe. She endured some serious pain.

But she's doing great in rehab. Joe smuggled me in one afternoon and we kissed and cuddled. She'll be home soon.

Meanwhile, I offered to "sub" for her this week.

I help, plus it gives me an opportunity to discuss some important issues with my pet "kinfolk" and Michele's readers.

As a "terrier activist," I watch for signs of human carelessness and neglect. Humans sometimes forget their obligations to their pets.

Ask your human for an early-spring vet check-up. Parasites seek warm and healthy cats and dogs to breed on during cold winter months. A blood test will reveal if you've been victimized by these dangerous critters and your vet can prescribe meds right away.

Dr. Johanna, my vet, recommends year-round maintenance doses of flea and tick prevention vaccines for me because we live in a woodsy, secluded area.

Deer get ticks that carry lyme disease (SHUDDER!). Fleas are mostly a pain in the tail, but can cause health trouble, too.

When you resume walking your human outdoors, remember to leash him and watch for other animals running loose. Some pets are bullies, and some forest creatures are just nasty.

A thick winter coat of fur is perfect for our 'hood, but spring grooming ROCKS! That bath feels sooo good, followed by a light trim and fluff.

I'm a sporty gal –no bows or braids for me- but I love my shiny new license. It cements Joe's and my relationship. I feel "engaged."

If your human is procrastinating, chew a slipper if you must (ones with Odor Eaters are actually pretty tasty) but get that license!

Joe is really conscientious about my welfare.

I LOVE when we brush my teeth. He buys special canine toothbrushes and toothpaste that's simply delicious! My tongue quivers when I swish that savory goop around my mouth.

Mmm-mmm! Beef-flavored mint toothpaste keeps me "moochie-fresh."

I took Joe to Central Park yesterday and we met a really HOT black Scotty male. His name is Newton. Isn't that *romantic*? Romeo, Casanova…Newton! Sigh!

He weighs 26 pounds but I like my men cuddly. We seemed to make a connection. Spring is wonderful!

I can't wait to tell Michele about him. She'll be back with you readers soon.

Till next time, wags and woofs to all.

LICORICE JOINS FACEBOOK

Hello, Readers! It's me, Licorice, Johnstown's canine correspondent. I asked Michele for her space today because I have exciting news. I joined Facebook!

I ruled out Instagram because I can't use cameras…that opposable thumb thing.

And Twitter? No thank you. First, what a ridiculous name! Folks who "tweet" sound foolish. I BARK! If they'd called it "Sniff" or "Fetch," I might have considered it.

Plus, writers can "chirp" only 140 words per post. That would stifle my creativity.

I'm fortunate to have mastered human communication skills. I depend on my First Amendment right to freedom of WOOF.

Since I reached middle age, I prefer intellectual pursuits to chasing balls or bunnies. Check out my vocabulary. I've been working crossword puzzles.

I'm still a terrier activist and registered voter. Facebook will connect me to my peers and alert me to their concerns.

Juno is Michele's God-dog (Michele helped name her). Her pet human is Eileen G. Juno fascinates me. Her human participates in many civic and charitable activities. Juno frequently attends community functions and always knows what's happening.

My cousin Cocoa can share family news with me.

Michele has a "second fur-cousin," Dusty. He travels a lot and promised to post photos of the seashore and other exciting vacation spots. Laura, his pet human, takes awesome pictures.

Facebook will open new doors for me. My tail is thumping (can you tell?).

Loretta O.'s grand-puppy, Phoebe, is an adorable Yorkie. We arfed by phone a week ago. When I told her she could learn human communication skills, she was thrilled. Her human, Therese, agreed to let me tutor Phoebe by computer and phone, sort of a K-12 canine home-schooling arrangement.

Jaxson's story bolsters my faith in miracles. Abandoned along the PA turnpike near Carlisle, Jaxson found his way to Jennifer L's front porch at 3 am. It was love at first wag. Jennifer adopted him immediately. Today he is clean, healthy, and happy.

At "Doggie-Daycare," Jax makes new friends, plays, snacks, and snoozes. Gam-Gam, his grand-human, moved to Myrtle Beach. Jax loves the beach and the ocean breezes tickling his ears.

"Ms. Kirby," a West Highland terrier, is a distant relative. She, too, has a pet human named Joe. She's glamorous, bright, and an accomplished pianist (see photo). Last spring she was a finalist in a local beauty pageant. She could easily become the first "Miss Canine America." I'm so looking forward to becoming better acquainted with her.

Michele welcomed my offer to fill in today. She's writing a book, a collection of her funniest columns. She plans to include some of my articles, too. I 'm sooo flattered.

Sad to say, seasonal changes loom ahead (crossword again!). Pet parents, be sure immunizations are up-to-date, and be certain your pooch is safe and warm when Mother Nature turns nasty. Petco sells washable, re-useable "PoochPads," perfect for avoiding dangerously frigid temperatures and deep snowfalls.

I enjoyed my opportunity to chat with you human readers today. Pet parents, love us the way we love you.

Wags and woofs to all.

LET'S MEET LICORICE! JOHNSTOWN MAGAZINE Q&A

Readers, thank you again for your warm responses and positive feedback regarding Johnstown Magazine's article about me this month.

However, JM believes they should have printed a Q & A featuring Licorice, our area's canine columnist. To help correct this oversight, I'm loaning my space to JM today. I'll catch ya next time, but for now, "Let's Meet Licorice."

JM: We're delighted to meet our first scholarly canine. How did you learn to read and write?

L: I picked up English by focusing intensely when humans spoke. Paper training presented an excellent opportunity to master reading skills. DogSpeak is our native tongue, but many of us can read, write, and communicate with humans.

JM: You look lovely. Is that hairstyle new?

L: Yes. Fur helps warm winters, but that April bath was heavenly. Spring grooming trends allow me to experiment and express myself as a woman. By the way, my human, Joe, gave me this glamorous hot pink halter/collar for Easter.

JM: Let's talk about Joe.

L: Joe rescued me. Unnoticed at the pet shop, breeders would have sent me off to produce endless litters. But Joe and I connected. We're both outdoorsy, casual, and unpretentious. I'm "fixed, "of course. But occasionally a hot male catches my eye. The aroma of "Hartz Mountain" is an aphrodisiac for me. But my heart belongs to Joe.

JM: You're described as a "terrier activist."

L: I woof loudly when I hear about animal abuse and neglect. So many heartless humans inflict unspeakable suffering on precious creatures who only want to love them. Pet parents must protect us.

JM: Do you consider yourself a "Scottish" American?
L: My heritage is Scottish, but I'm all-American. My proudest moment came when Joe took me to vote the first time. A lady marked my paw print in her book, and I presented my license as ID. Voting is serious business, but I believe I have good scents.

JM: You appear fearless, Licorice. Does anything frighten you?
L: Our nation becomes more violent every day. People, and some critters, too, don't value life as the gift it is. Humans and animals are senselessly bullied, abused, wounded, even killed.

Joe tethers me in our yard and on our porch for my protection. Our neighborhood is woodsy, and sometimes I get tempted to chase a bunny or scare a deer (I'm ashamed to admit that). Joe lets me walk him on our leash for his safety. Humans are unpredictable; owning one is a significant responsibility.

One evening, while I napped soundly on the porch, Joe walked to a neighbor's on a quick errand.

I woke up to a THUD. Two huge Dobermans snarled at me menacingly. Then, they pounced. Biting and gouging, they tore my fur and skin. Trapped on my own porch, I yelped helplessly in horrific pain.

Then, they were gone. I tried to stand, but couldn't. Bloody wounds and gashes covered my 13 lb body.

Suddenly, Joe appeared. He wrapped me in a blanket and rushed me my vet. I happily recognized Dr. Johanna right away. I trust her to take care of me.

That night, I heard scary words no pooch should EVER hear: traumatic ruptures, internal injuries, splenectomy, operate immediately. It took a long time for me to heal, but Joe demonstrated excellent nursing skills.

JM: WOW! As we conclude, what would you like to say to our readers?
L: Warm weather's coming. Every season brings perils to animals and humans alike. Parasites rule summer. Make sure you immunize us all year long. Humans…are you up-to-date with tetanus and Lyme disease vaccines?

Let's take shorter walks in shadier places during cooler hours. Joe turned 60. Gotta watch blood pressure, over-exertion. We canines are caregivers, too.

Carry a water bottle. And NEVER leave us in a hot car! Responsibility goes beyond purchasing licenses, getting shots, and scooping. Humans, love us unconditionally, the way we love you.

CHAPTER 10: MISSIN' THE OLD DAYS

WAIT! DON'T PUT ME ON *HOLD* !

Naughty bankers invented "pin numbers" in the mid 70's to drive depositors crazy. Bored managers laid off dozens of tellers, replacing them with ATM machines.

Tellers would politely ask, "May I help you?"

Machines said, "Beep."

The concept spread like wild fire. Soon, credit card companies, utilities, online mail order, and social networks followed suit. They insisted that customers have pin numbers or passwords.

I'm not a "number kinda" gal. Personally, I preferred passwords. "Abra Cadabra, " "Open Sesame,"...that's classy.

Hubby and I once shared the same pin on our bank account. When my "ex" exited, a circuit blew!

A clerk at our bank announced," You know you'll need a new pin," my steaming eyeballs could barely read the dial gizmo.

"May I select a word instead?" I inquired.

I do my best work when I'm enraged. The word I chose is unacceptable for a family newspaper, but I can tell you it brought a smile to my lips each time I visited the "drive-thru" for 12 years.

My garage door security system also required a pin. A delicate, sensitive system, it malfunctioned if the moon was full or a raccoon burped in a nearby yard.

I used up my birthday, old addresses, my odometer reading, and church envelope number when the technician repeatedly reprogrammed it. By then, he and I were on first name terms.

"Another number?" I sighed. "Hon, what year did you graduate?"
"1976," he replied.

That magic number made the door behave for 8 years until I threw a hissy fit and "banished" someone from my world. I outdid myself with fury that time, picking an "un-Trib-able" but totally unforgettable (to those privy to it) word.

A cartoon I saw on FaceBook showed St Peter at his Heavenly desk informing a new arrival, "I'm sorry, but your user name doesn't match your password."

I can't count how many times I've heard those words.

I'm not some old bat who drools and talks to furniture (on my way, but not there yet!) and I get genuinely insulted when some patronizing operator gently asks me if I REMEMBER my mother's maiden name.

I now record "pins and passies" in a booklet with addresses, birthdays, phone numbers, and other info, safe in a Ziploc stashed under…OOPS, can't tell ya.

YOU don't have security clearance. If you found and compromised my book, forcing me to make up all new "passies," I'd have to hurt you.

I got it! I'll give YOU a password!

It must include 3 capital letters, a Roman numeral, your blood type, a gang tattoo, and 2 digits from your license plate.

What? No car? No plate? I have to call a supervisor. Let me put you on hold.

DAZZLE YOUR LADY

I saw a joke on the Internet recently: Instructions on How to Please Women. It listed 5 simple steps: take her to dinner; buy her jewelry; pretend to share her interests; love her; die for her.

The punchline was How to Please Men: dress like a Kardashian and bring beer.

These suggestions sounded extreme. I don't need pricey trinkets or lavish meals. I *certainly* don't need anyone to die for me.

I believe that often men take women for granted. "She loves me," they declare confidently, and expect us to tolerate sloth, lethargy, apathy, and indifference.

"Why are you single?" too many folks ask me. "You're bright, creative, appealing."

"I'm overqualified," I reply.

But…SINCE YOU ASKED, here are "Reasonable and Sensible Ways to Please Me."

1. Teeth. I like teeth, original or after-market. They should be clean and accompanied by minty-fresh breath.

2. Hair I'm fond of hair (again, original or synthetic) but it must be clean locks combed neatly. Unnatural colors (blues, pinks) or bizarre "do's" (Mohawks, bald with tattoos) are deal breakers.

3. Wardrobe There's the "favorite shirt": frayed sleeves, ring-around-the-collar, and a mystery stain unresponsive to Shout, Lestoil, Oxyclean, and turpentine.

a. The little polo pony jumped ship years ago, not wanting to tarnish the IZOD reputation. Set the shirt free. It may wax a car someday.

b. Let's talk shoes. If only for safety, they should be in one piece. Black socks do NOT look good with sneakers. They look even worse with sandals. In ANY "Last Supper" reproduction you've ever seen, did you spot an apostle wearing socks with sandals? (I *think* it's a Commandment!)

4. Be a "DO BEE"! (Remember "Romper Room"?)

Do you know what the Dirt Devil looks like? Spend a few quality moments with it after you spill coffee grounds or when you finish trimming your toenails.

Have you ever wondered what's in those Clorox and Lysol canisters next to the sinks? Be adventurous! Recklessly pop one of those strange, baffling wipes out and see what happens. When you boldly attack toothpaste smears, coffee rings, messy crumbs or tiny hairs, armed with mere disinfectant...It's MAGIC!

5. I don't expect expensive, eye-popping jewelry. My eyes would pop if I saw my hero replacing an empty bathroom spool with a fluffy, new roll of Cottonelle..

6. Love me. Make me laugh. Hug me. Remind me of the freedom and silliness of the youth we shared. Take me to a club to hear a band, or let's go watch a chick flick at the drive-in.

An evening at Walmart is NOT a date.

Wanna please me (or one of dozens of women reading this)? It's not so hard. Ya think?

Everybody's life tells a story. Every story has a soundtrack. Make sure yours rocks!

SA SHEWS ON DA ARDOR FOUTE

Sa Shews on Da Arder Foute
Readers, I didn't snap. Work with me, ok?

Nicholas (grandpa on my Dad's side), Ivan and George sailed from Croatia at ages 15 and 16. They landed at Ellis Island, followed the rules, and became documented immigrants.

It humbles me to imagine the barriers they encountered: language, transportation, housing. These teens (un-tattooed, un-pierced, wearing underwear that fit) courageously journeyed to foreign soil to pursue their dreams.

I have enduring respect for my Croatian ancestors, and all others who trek legally to faraway lands seeking education, adventure and success.

I want to know how the folks with below minimal English skills end up working in Customer Service. Who's in charge of Human Resources...Elmer Fudd?

I usually play nicely with recorded personnel. I prefer ones who ask me to press 1 for yes and 2 for no. They are efficient; they don't display snarky attitudes; they are re-chargeable; and they speak impeccable English.

"Thank you for choosing Expressive Fashion Footwear. Our menu has changed. To place new orders, press 1; billing questions, press 2..." I listened patiently.

Then, he asked me a question. No recorded person EVER asked me a question without giving me choices. "Explain your reason for calling today."

I was speechless, and YOU know how often THAT happens!

Why was I calling? Because I ordered a pair of blue 10W sneakers, and the box that arrived contained only 1 shoe (I could NOT MAKE THIS STUFF UP).

"I did not hear your response. Please repeat." The recorded man was getting testy.

I knew what I had to say. "Customer Service."

The words would first send me to "Hold Purgatory," where innocent customers must forcibly listen to music reminiscent of when the lid from the chicken soup fell down the disposal. The music is interrupted every 20 seconds by a voice who reminds me how important my call is. At least 30 minutes of my life is forever wasted.

Suddenly, the music stops. A stern-sounding female "recordette" states "This call may be recorded for training and education purposes." Oh, please! Record it! Record it!

"Cushtomar Srvishe. I am Fehtgm Dyxupo. Zipch code, prease. ...phone nummer, prease. Prease confirm home addresh. OK, how may I misunderstand you and make you crazy today?"

OK, he didn't say that, but you know it's coming.

"You ardared jus 1 shew?"

"No. I ordered a pair. 2. I have 2 feet. 2 shoes!" I replied.

"May I have ardar nummer prease?"

"Certainly. NXB8395KPLM-2XLVFYN."

"Ardar say 2 shew sent."

"Well, only 1 shoe arrived," I sighed. "Maybe the other 1 took a walk."

"Ha! Ha! You funny lady! Did you receipt a right or left?"

"What difference does it make?" I snarled. "Please send me another pair of blue sneakers in size 10W."

"You need pay ship and handle cause this not return."

"Whatever," I sighed.

Today was Tuesday. The sun shone brightly. Apparently, Mother Nature went back on her meds. I decided to treat myself. I hopped in the car and cruised to Burger King. I LOVE "cheesy tots."

I drove to the screen. "1 cheesy tots, please."

"Izzat...buzz..static...all?" crackled the speaker.

"Oh, I'll take a Diet Coke, too."

UBERS AND LIZARDS AND DEER! OH, MY!

Picture this:

You're motoring down the road. Your ride, a "beater," is all your budget allows. You purchased your insurance from a lizard.

CRASH!

Scene 1 Auto vs Auto. If you are the "whacker," liability protects you. Your beater is history, but the lizard will repair or replace the "whackee's" vehicle. No hard feelings, right?

Oh, are you injured? Tsk! Tsk! Bites to be you. If you're the "whackee," utter a quick prayer that your whacker didn't shop with the lizard, too. Even worse, the driver may not have purchased insurance anywhere, from anyone, ever; nor does he possess a license.

This stellar citizen drove under the radar for six, maybe seven, years.

If the secret citizen suffered any boo boo, he/she probably has a personal injury attorney on speed dial.

If *you're* hurt, see above-mentioned prayer.

Scene 2 Deer vs Auto (We DO live in PA, y'know!)

You perform a rapid injury assessment. The airbag deployed; no broken bones. But you'll feel the bruises tomorrow. You didn't go through the windshield.

You ask yourself, "Self, should I get out of the car?"

Bambi's uncle, downwind of a frisky doe, never saw you coming. Now, he's apparently vanished, leaving a nasty-looking chunk of bloody antler wedged behind your wipers. Your vehicle, covered from moon roof to hubcaps in dense, sticky fur, is still purring (Sorry. Couldn't help myself!).

LEAVE the scene. It's not like "Uncle Rack" plans to call the cops and file a complaint. He won't phone your insurance agent, either.

Retreat to a nearby pull-off area and examine your car. Is it still roadsafe? Tires intact? Broken glass? Oil or gas leaks? No? You can make it home.

Your heart wants to return to the "crime scene." NOT a good idea.

If Unc crawled off to die, guilt will overwhelm you when you find the body.

Suppose he didn't die? Manly antlers arouse does. He now sports half-a-rack, is probably bald and itching for revenge. GO HOME!

Don't tidy your car. Yes, folks observing the damage will whisper and laugh. However, statistics prove that insurance companies frequently question deer-related claims. (Google it! I did!)

Scene 3. You're heading to a Steeler home game and notice that the car passing you has NO DRIVER! The car door displays a "Uber" logo, and the passenger in the backseat is napping.

Scary? You Betcha!.

Uber introduced driverless cars in Pittsburgh in September 2016. They based their strategy on the fact that autos in Pittsburgh already seem driverless, and no one would notice.

The Federal Highway Act of 1968 made seatbelts mandatory. Blind Spot, Forward Collision and Rear Cameras warn drivers of potential dangers either visually (flashing lights) or audibly (beeping).

Actually, the auto industry has been "uberizing" vehicles for quite a while. Cruise control, air bags, and self-parking are marketed as safety features.

Robotic cars find one obstacle insurmountable: Mankind! Idiotic human divers often make chaotic maneuvers that defy logic.

One CEO stated, "No software developed as of now can reliably operate a vehicle without a cautious human supervising."

Auto robotics is currently perfecting "auto-to driver" and "auto-to-auto" communication.

We already have "idiot lights":" Blinkie, Blinkie. You are out of gas"; "Blinkie, Blinkie, no oil. Your motor just burned up."

Frankly, I object to my car "dissin' me." As for YOU and YOUR car dissin' me, I prefer to swear or flip the bird. Auto-robotics will just have to wait for me to evolve.

ABOUT THE AUTHOR

Michele Mikesic Bender is a retired high school English teacher from Johnstown, PA. Currently, she writes a bi-monthly humor column on Sundays for the Johnstown Tribune Democrat. A very active senior citizen in spite of a handicap, she vividly recalls her baby-boomer exploits and continues to live her life to the fullest.

Made in the USA
Middletown, DE
29 December 2019